T0343638

"An enlightening guide to redefining masculinity through effective communication. *The Art of Conscious Communication for Thoughtful Men* brings a refreshing perspective to the modern man, helping him navigate conversations with empathy, clarity, and respect."

—Scott Jeffrey Miller, seven-time bestselling author and host of the world's largest weekly leadership podcast

The Art of

CONSCIOUS COMMUNICATION

for
Thoughtful
Men

The Art of

CONSCIOUS COMMUNICATION

for
Thoughtful
Men

Effective Personal and Professional
Communication Skills

JEM FULLER

CORAL GABLES

For permission requests, please contact the publisher at:

Mango Publishing Group

2850 S Douglas Road, 2nd Floor

Coral Gables, FL 33134 USA

info@mango.bz

For special orders, quantity sales, course adoptions and corporate sales, please email the publisher at sales@mango.bz. For trade and wholesale sales, please contact Ingram Publisher Services at customer.service@ ingramcontent.com or +1.800.509.4887.

The Art of Conscious Communication for Thoughtful Men: Effective Personal and Professional Communication Skills

Library of Congress Cataloging-in-Publication number: 2024936416

ISBN: (p) 978-1-68481-596-8 (e) 978-1-68481-597-5

BISAC category code BUS107000, BUSINESS & ECONOMICS / Personal Success

First published in Australia in 2021 by KMD Books Waikiki, WA 6169

www.kmdbooks.com

The information provided in this book is based on the research, insights, and experiences of the author. Every effort has been made to provide accurate and up-to-date information; however, neither the author nor the publisher warrants the information provided is free of factual error. This book is not intended to diagnose, treat, or cure any medical condition or disease, nor is it intended as a substitute for professional medical care. All matters regarding your health should be supervised by a qualified healthcare professional. The author and publisher disclaim all liability for any adverse effects arising out of or relating to the use or application of the information or advice provided in this book.

With thanks and love to Talia

Written for Jedi and Noah

Contents

PART IV—PAYING IT FORWARD

PROLOGUE

The undercurrent of anger was very quickly swelling toward an explosion of mob violence. I didn't know what had caused it and didn't have time to find out. The two Japanese tourists in the center of the rapidly growing circle of outraged, tribal Pakistani men, looked dazed and confused, as fear now consumed and gripped them.

We were on the mob's turf. Three foreigners deep in the Hindu Kush mountains of remote North Pakistan. 1998. Tribal law. Kalashnikovs. Isolated dirt mountain roads on the sides of vertical cliffs. Endless valleys and crevasses, where unfortunates could go missing, never to be found. I was aware of the two tourists on the bus, but hadn't interacted with them. I was trying to blend in. They were standing out. I was in local clothing, they were in shorts, tank tops, and flip-flops. I knew where I was. They had thought they were in Disneyland, an illusion that was now very quickly falling apart.

I rushed in, putting myself between the ringleaders and the Japanese boys. I can't remember exactly what I said to the locals, but the extent of my Urdu was very limited, so it would've been something along the lines of, "Please sirs, one minute sirs, please wait. I'll speak with them. No problems. Please relax. One minute."

Then, with an adequate amount of urgency, I ushered the Japanese boys toward the bus and the women and children before returning to the infuriated men to keep the dialogue open with them.

Through the next fifteen minutes of listening, appeasing, and appealing, I found out what had happened (thanks to one of the younger men, who was a university student and spoke some English). At the border crossing from China into Pakistan, when the bus had stopped for a break, the Japanese guys thought it would be funny to take photos of each other with their pants down, bent over and "mooning" for the camera—next to the "Welcome to Pakistan" sign! Really? Oh dear.

The patriotic and conservative locals were understandably incensed. The ignorant tourists were confused. Wasn't "flashing a moon" a funny, slightly risqué thing to do we've seen in American teen movies? Yeah, maybe in California, dudes, not remote North Pakistan, for crying out loud!

A massive misunderstanding. A vast divide of difference. Almost no ability to communicate, save for this one Aussie who luckily happened to be on that bus with a handful of Urdu words.

Suffice to say, no one got shot and thrown off a cliff. I pulled the boys aside for some stern words of advice—"You're not in Kansas anymore" kind of stuff. Pay some respect, put some appropriate clothes on, perhaps even learn how to say "*As-salaamu alaikum.*" You could even read up a bit on the culture and background of where you are, if you really wanted to knock yourselves out! Just make some effort to communicate respect.

In the absence of communication, there is only disconnect and distance. There can be no collaboration, no communion, no resolution. In that void, we perish.

So Much More

Communication is so much more than just the exchange of information. It is the bridge over the divide of difference. It is the way to reconciliation and the road to making a better world. It is the thread between isolation and connection. It is also the tool with which we manifest our creations from ideas into reality. Communication underpins our ability to collaborate and solve the biggest problems.

More personally, it is also the foundation of the quality of our relationships, and this constitutes the quality of our experience of life. Our ability to be effective in any situation is intrinsically linked to our ability to communicate.

And yet we do not teach our emerging young adults the finer art of Conscious Communication. In fact, in lots of cultures, we teach our men, especially, to *not* communicate; to "deal with it and stay strong" with a "stiff upper lip" and to hide their feelings. "Don't cry like a girl!" "Suck it up!" "Grin and bear it, son!"

Could this be part of the reason internal tensions build in males and then finally explode through anger and aggression? Or result in avoidance, detachment, and numbness? Although the general male propensity toward aggression can be argued to have evolved due to needing to compete for reproductive success and then "protect the tribe," it would appear that we needlessly propagate this tendency in a dysfunctional way due to the constraints and pressures of cultural stereotypes.

It's time to break free from the shackles of antiquity and continue to evolve. It's time to redefine. It's time to improve as men.

What Is "Conscious Communication"?

The more conscious we are of something, the more aware of it we are. The more conscious we are of communication itself—the purpose, the subtleties and nuances, the flavors and features, and the people involved—the better we can be at our part in it; better as a listener seeking to understand, or as a speaker hoping to be understood.

The ability to maintain high-level acuity (keenness of perception), and remain present and engaged at the same time, is an art and a practice that can be improved as a skill. Preparation for upcoming, planned communication can greatly enhance the degree of success. Knowing why, what, how, and with whom you are communicating aids in the form and quality of delivery.

Even when we find ourselves in spontaneous, unplanned communication, the ability to steady ourselves, to slow down and come to a place of calm awareness, greatly assists us in being present to the communication. We are more available to the sharing of information, instructions, ideas, emotions, or even just energy. Conscious Communication is more mindful communication. Conscious Communication is being more aware of yourself, of others, and of the bigger picture. Conscious Communication is an act of service.

Some Foundational Conscious Comms Pillars

1. The responsibility for successful communication is with the communicator (the one with the information to share). Are you speaking just to hear the sound of your own voice, or do you have something you actually need to have understood by others? Learn how to adjust your delivery depending on the context and the person, or people, you are communicating with.

2. The art of listening and seeking to understand is vital for Conscious Communication.

3. The communication itself is more important than the individuals involved.

4. Intention is paramount. Make sure your intention is good. If you are coming from a good place, all will be well. When it's time to speak your truth, do so with love.

The Process: Why–Who–What–How–When–Pause–Share

In this book I will explain, in detail, a process I have created and outlined here. It is designed to be used for communication you are intending to have, not for spontaneous conversation. The first part of this process is actually a good way to decide whether it's best to communicate what you're thinking or feeling at all.

- Step 1: Why? For what purpose? What are you hoping for from this communication? If your intention is good and you are aiming for a net sum positive outcome, i.e., for the greater good of all concerned, that's a strong indication to communicate.

- Step 2: Who? Think about the person or people you will be communicating with. Consider them as you design your delivery.

- Step 3: What? Ultimately, what is it you want to communicate? Start with the end in mind.

- Step 4: How? There are many ways to communicate something. Choose the one you think will best serve the situation.

- Step 5: When? Timing is critical. Pick the wrong moment, and your communication may not only fall short, but even cause adverse reactions.

- Step 6: Pause. The time has come; you are about to communicate your message. Take a moment to pause, breathe, and come into your center.

- Step 7: Share. Do your thing! Communication is an act of service. When you frame it like this, it's easier to do.

Generalizations

For the purpose of illustrating the ideas in this book, it is necessary for me to generalize. Of course, there are a multitude of variations and versions of the human behavioral patterns I discuss. We are, as a species, beautifully complex creatures (yes, even "simple men"), and we exist moving along the spectrums between the poles of the apparent dualities of life. We can be at either end, or anywhere between, and this can always be changing.

I would not, however, be able to communicate concisely if, at every turn, I had to keep excusing myself for not including all possible anomalies. My hope is that you will find parts of this book illustrated through the generalizations that resonate with you, and then use these understandings to elevate your own experience of communication and your relationship with life.

This book is not a scientific paper. It is simply a sharing of stories, experiences, and strategies in the hope that some of what is written here will help make your life easier.

Part I

YOU AND COMMS

Chapter One

AN OUTBURST

Most people on the Thai beach that night had no idea the brawl that was about to erupt had been brewing within the small gang of local young men for a few weeks. My wife and I knew. We knew the men, the youngest of whom, at sixteen, was only a boy, and the primary protagonist for the horrible, violent fight that was about to take place. Lucky was his name.

In the month leading up to this night, I had been tattooing some of the group members up at their Rasta Bar, a tree house reggae restaurant and hangout venue for backpackers on the island. Through my gifting of time and ink and art, I had gained the respect and protection of the gang.

Payback for a prior incident, a decent amount of Thai amphetamines, and local whiskey and beer fueled Lucky and his older tribe members down to the backpackers' beach party around a fire that night. There were about one hundred travelers lying around on the sand, drinking, smoking pot, and listening to music.

Lucky threw a beer bottle at someone's head. Within minutes, it was on. Ten high and angry Thais trying to kick and punch the shit out of everyone they could. People were screaming and scampering everywhere. It was when I saw an innocent girl, trying to stand peacefully in the way, get punched in the face that I had to get involved. Remove the linchpin, I remember thinking.

I ran through the brawl, picked Lucky up over my shoulder and kept running. I took him away from the action, around the back of some bungalows, and pinned him to the sand in a bear hug restraint. The boy who had been whimpering and crying under my tattoo needles weeks before was now kicking and screaming like a lunatic, desperate to be back in the fray.

Without him there, the brawl soon dissipated, and people retreated to their accommodations. Lucky's older brother, also wild that night, was threatening to kill me, and as I chaperoned Lucky with a tight grip back toward his tree house, the brother and I faced off on the beach, standing toe to toe. After a few seconds of locked eyes, he backed down and let me pass with Lucky. Thank fuck for that. I'm a pacifist, and he was a dangerous man.

Resorting to violence was all these boys knew. Even the concept of being able to communicate their emotions and talk through their problems before eruptions become inevitable would've been completely foreign to them. To lots of men. In lots of cultures. It's time we learnt better ways.

The Art of Conscious Communication for Thoughtful Men

Even with their misguided frustrations and anger, Lucky and his Thai brothers were bonded together. They would fight for each other, and were inseparable (until Lucky got taken off the island to spend some time in jail). They weren't blood brothers; they found each other and formed a tribe, a family of sorts. All for one, one for all. "At least I'm not alone."

There is good reason for the deep-seated human fear of isolation; our evolution and survival has been largely due to our socialization, our connection and community, our ability to communicate. Even though psychological and even physical isolation is but a very seemingly real illusion, it can still bring about the death of our "soul," extinguishing our spirit and diminishing our will to live.

The fact is that, as long as we breathe in air, eat food, and drink water, we remain inextricably connected to and a part of all life, recycling and regenerating the same atoms and energy as each other and all things (from the same stardust building blocks). Despite this very real connection, the power of perceived isolation can be our demise. This is true even for the stoic and "lone wolf" male.

More broadly, our ability to share new concepts, to inspire and motivate, to influence and lead, and to listen and comprehend, is in our ability to communicate. Interpersonal abilities such as rapport, collaboration, partnership, teamwork, intimacy, and love all fall over when communication fails. The deepest connections become glitchy over a time of perpetual misunderstandings.

~~~~

Unfortunately, the abuse of honest communication is also a tool used in the divisive endeavors of those set to destroy harmony. In our modern day, the deliberate and sometimes algorithmic spreading of false information is being used to undermine our trust in honest institutions, in each other, and in the structures of our society. As much as communication can be the manifestation of the wonders of genius, in the wrong hands and in the viral spread of social media, it can be used to start riots and wars.

Most impasses, conflicts, and interpersonal dysfunction are due to miscommunication. There are also many things that don't get said (despite it being in the best interest of the "greater good") for fear of confrontation, or honest conversations going pear-shaped.

The challenges and hurdles to better, more effective interpersonal communication can be hard to navigate, especially as they are largely invisible and misunderstood. These hurdles lie camouflaged in the intricate web of the human behavioral code. People are often completely confounded as to why their communication has been so misinterpreted.

We are prone to take much of what we hear personally and distort the information, as we filter it through our lens of bias and belief. Most of us (regardless of gender) have not been taught the deeper skills of pausing and not "acting on our reactions." We have not been taught how to create the space to be curious in our listening and thus expand the range of response options.

We are not educated in school on how to read others' "behavioral styles" (see Chapter Fifteen) or "love languages" (see Gary Chapman's books). There are no classes on ego or identity and how they can get in the way of clear communication. Only in recent years have schools started to include mindfulness practices and teach our next generation how to remain present in the moment, which can be the beginning of more mindful and conscious communication.

There are many aspects of communication that add complexity to any situation, based on the context and purpose of the comms in question. For example, if the purpose of the conversation were to strengthen the bond between two people, then the conscious approach to that moment would be different than if the purpose were to effectively communicate specific instructions.

———

The art of Conscious Communication can certainly be learnt, practiced, and improved. It is a deeply personal and, dare I say, spiritual journey of self-discovery, self-acceptance, and elevation beyond the unconscious and reactionary realm of ego and fear. This then leads to the experience of larger consciousness, curiosity, the untapped depth of connection, and the truest sense of the greater good.

Conscious Communication is about getting out of your own way (not making it all about you), and truly *seeing* those with whom you are communicating. Through learning this art, men can evolve and expand beyond the restrictions of stereotype, becoming better partners, fathers, friends, and influencers.

More largely, I believe the art of Conscious Communication is integral to saving the human race from deteriorating into the dysfunctional abyss of fear-based identity politics and "shouting at each other" from across the divides. To come closer, again, to the reality of us actually being of the same species, on the same planet, with the same resources.

As we all, one by one, become less defensive and "lean in" to curiosity, listening and seeking to understand, we will improve the quality of our discourse. As we learn ways to communicate our deepest truths, and allow ourselves to accept our own vulnerabilities, we can rewrite the negative gender stereotype, and all become better men.

The art of Conscious Communication is an imperative part of the way forward for us all. And it starts with you.

Chapter Two

YOU DON'T NEED TO BE AN ISLAND

I had retreated again. Even as I stood there with her still in the room, I was rowing my escape boat farther away. My internal world was yet again a swirling sea of emotions I could barely understand, let alone communicate. And what was the point? I'd probably fuck it up. My mouth would go dry, and I would just sound angry. She would take it the wrong way, again, turn my words around and accuse me of something or other. Better to be accused of shutting her out and "being an island." At least it was quiet and calm in solitude.

And anyway (I justified to myself), I'm not shutting her out, I'm letting her have it her way. Besides, arguing and speaking rudely to each other is pointless to me—completely unproductive and unenjoyable. Let's just agree to disagree and leave each other alone. Shut it down. Suck it up. Crack a beer and get on with things. (Oh dear!) Yet somehow deep inside I knew, or at least hoped, I could be a better man in relationships—that a better relationship was possible. I hadn't gotten to the point of giving up on us. Not yet. But I didn't know what I could work on to do better. "It takes two to tango" kept ringing loudly in my ears, and it felt like one of us wanted to salsa instead.

The questions kept turning over and over. Was it really unsavable? Unfixable? Had the river of resentment become such an unstoppable force that nothing could curb its inevitable flow to the sea of separation? Apparently so. The more desperately I held on with clenched fists, the more it all slipped painfully between my fingers and out of reach.

As I write and look back now, with the benefit of hindsight and knowing stuff I simply didn't know, I realize many things about myself—about my version of a man-who-knew-no-better. I hadn't known how to access my own calm whilst remaining present and available for her through turbulence. I didn't know how to park my ego and not take things so personally, or how to not bite back defensively. I didn't understand (let alone honor!) her natural ability to dance so nimbly through the chaos of such quickly changing emotional states.

I also didn't know how to change the common denominator of all my relationships—me. Despite the varying degrees of openness in communication with other people, with my deeper vulnerabilities, I was still an island. Even in my most trusted relationships with my siblings and closest friends, due to shame and a subconscious belief of not being enough, I kept my saddest, secret tortures completely to myself. It turns out there's no healing possible when you're on the island all alone.

Don't get me wrong—I'm not suggesting anyone will, or can, come and save you. Your liberation from any personal suffering is yours alone to work on. I'm just saying that opening up and sharing what you're going through is an important part of the healing process. This is a form of Conscious Communication.

One of the things I've learnt in the last decade of my life is that, when you start building bridges between your island-of-deepest-vulnerabilities and others, you realize you're not alone, and that you certainly don't need to stay stuck. At the core of my past shame was that, through the years of one of my pivotal partnerships, I had developed severe anxieties around having sex, to the point of almost complete dysfunction. What I desperately wanted to communicate was, "I adore you and honor you and want to pleasure you!" "I am your man, and I can take you like no other!" "I am invincible, and I am in control!" The tragedy was that my fears of not being good enough manifested as a gripping psychological racket that had me showing up as the opposite: "weak," "self-consumed," "anxious," "out of control," and completely unable to "be her man" in that way.

When I finally had the courage to start sharing this struggle, my road to healing began. I commenced the journey of "rewiring" my self-belief, beginning a daily practice of self-acceptance and self-love. As I changed my internal world, my relationship to the outside world changed as well. The desperation dissolved, the desire remained, and I gave myself the redemptive gift of another chance at love. It is with a large dose of Relief, a big dollop of Joy, and a few loud "Woohoos!!" that I can say I now have zero shame and enjoy fully functional lovemaking ability, and those crippling anxieties, thankfully, are no longer a part of my life.

If you have anything that you still keep tucked away under a blanket of your own shame, you will become lighter and more liberated in the communication of it. Whether you share it in the intimacy of a close and trusted relationship, or in the air of a more open forum (like a men's group[1]*, or a "conscious conversations" group[2]**), you will enjoy the benefits all the same.

Even if you feel resolved with all your "stuff," sharing your own experience of shame, struggle, embarrassment, guilt, etc., may very well be serving those who hear it. Quite often another person will be suffering in their version of your story, and you may just be opening a door and shining a light to freedom for them to walk toward.

---

1 *Men's group—there are formal and organized groups of men who come together to help each other grow personally. Look them up online and you'll find them. I sit with some men in my community around a fire each month and we take turns to communicate where we are at. We pick a theme to talk about each month. Look up "men's circle work" for info on that.

2 **Conscious conversations group—a friend of mine and I decided to host a donation-to-charity evening each month in which I facilitate groups of people to come together and talk about important and meaningful subjects. It's quite straightforward to organize, and everyone who attends has expressed gratitude for the opportunity to share their thoughts and to hear what others think or feel. We need to have conversations about stuff that matters.

The Poles of Apparent Duality (AD)

It seems appropriate now to write about the apparent dualities that we perceive in aspects of life, mainly because I will reference this phenomenon consistently as a theme through the chapters of this book—and because I have just alluded to one. By apparent duality, I mean two things that are seemingly opposing, yet not only do they coexist, without each other, they don't exist (halves of a whole). You are not an island, and yet at the same time, your experience of life is yours alone and no one can truly know what it is to be you.

~~~~

"Oooooh, I'd love to go to Cappadocia! Can I come with you?" she asked excitedly over the din of downtown streets in Istanbul.

I tried to reply as respectfully as possible. "Of course, you can get on the same bus as me, and I am happy to hang out and chat. I do, however, want to let you know that I'm traveling solo these days. The alone time I have is really important to me." Silence.

"Oh, okay. Sure."

She didn't get on the bus. She may well have taken it personally, even though that's not at all how it was meant. It's interesting how humans react to each other wanting some time alone. "Have I done something wrong?" "Was it something I said?"

For me, it wasn't about her. I would have said the same thing to anyone else. I was genuinely enjoying my time alone. Exploring the quieter, unknown regions of myself, becoming familiar with my own quirks and idiosyncrasies, making peace within. It is this "alone work" that rests as the other half of curating our capacity for functional connection with others and with life.

Previously, I spoke about the benefits of building bridges with communication, so that you are not an island in terms of your feelings and vulnerabilities. Yet, at the same time, it is also very healthy to maintain an independent sense of self, to be self-reliant and self-sustaining. You need not be alone, *and* you are alone and solely responsible at the same time. Apparent duality. The two coexist and breathe life into each other. The health of one is the health of the other.

You are inextricably linked and connected to all life, literally and inescapably, within the greater system of things. Yet, at the same time, in your perception of being here, you are entirely alone. I find it helpful to remember this in times of strife. Acceptance of both truths creates the opportunity to relax into whatever your current place on the spectrum may be.

I use the term "apparent duality" (and will also refer to it using the acronym AD), because, although it's easy to see opposites everywhere we look in life, beyond this human perspective, duality is an illusion—the halves are of the whole. There is a bigger reality: that everything is ultimately of one, same, unified field. But that is a fascinating and mysterious, philosophical/ quantum-physical topic for other books.

Apparent duality (AD) has been most beautifully represented in the famous Chinese symbol, yin and yang. We find AD everywhere: day and night, feminine and masculine, northern and southern hemisphere, happy and sad, functional and dysfunctional, and so on. In fact, a beautiful and fundamental AD exists at the very place from which we experience anything and everything: our brain. Our right and left hemispheres are separate (joined primarily by the corpus callosum). They have different functions and can be successfully mutually exclusive. In fact, fascinating experiments with split brain and stroke patients show that each hemisphere can have its own "personality" and conscious awareness. AD at the very center of our experience! (For fascinating further reading on this, look up the work of Dr. Iain McGilchrist.)

This AD of things is actually a spectrum from one end to the other, with a gradient blending on the scale between. For example, with day and night, it's not just one or the other. It's not that it's just day, then instantly the light switches off and it's night. There is every shade of dusk and dawn in each transition, and while it is day somewhere, it must be night somewhere else. Similarly, we are not always either completely happy or sad. Sometimes we just feel neutral, or even happy about something and sad about something else simultaneously! We certainly are complex creatures.

When I work with leaders, we talk about how leadership is not about you. It's a role of service; you are there to lead for the benefit of others, the greater good. At the same time, however, leadership is about you, because you are the leader! AD— it's about you inasmuch as it's about your ability to get out of the way and not make it about you! This is very similar in Conscious Communication.

Exploring what each end of any duality is for you will help you access each pole to your advantage and allow you to move between the two to communicate more effectively. Having a greater awareness of each end of any spectrum enables you to be more conscious of where you are at given points in time as well. Becoming more self-aware is the first step toward self-mastery.

In the next chapter, we will discover how developing more Conscious Communication starts with the relationship you have with yourself. It's about others, and it's about you.

Functional and Dysfunctional

I prefer to look at the different ways of thinking, behaving, communicating, action-taking, and so on in terms of how functional or dysfunctional they are, rather than there being a "right" or a "wrong" way to do something. Saying that there is a right or wrong way for people to think or feel is fraught with potential for moral judgement, shame, chastising, separation, misunderstanding, condemnation, and so on. When the purpose is to communicate effectively, I find it better to leave those terms aside and go with "functional" or "dysfunctional."

Functional simply means it achieved the purpose in a healthy, sustainable, and resourceful way. Good for you, good for those around you—net sum impact, positive. Communication successful. Dysfunctional means that it didn't achieve the outcome or purpose. It wasn't necessarily good for you, or those around you—net sum impact, negative. Communication unsuccessful.

Within all of the ways we can understand ourselves, some of which I am sharing in this book, it appears there can be functional and dysfunctional versions of the same pattern (and every variant on the spectrum between).

How do we know if the way we communicated was functional or not? Asking these questions might help you know.

- Did you achieve the purpose?

- If you wanted someone to feel loved, did it work?

- If you wanted someone to understand how you feel, did it work?

- If you were trying to explain a complex process, did the other person come to understand?

- Was your method of communication sustainable, or was it draining?

- Could you keep up this approach in similar situations, or does it wear you out?

You will see, as we explore human patterns in communication, that a degree of functionality or dysfunctionality can be observed in all of them. My invitation to you is to practice loving self-inquiry as you learn new ways to communicate. Notice what works for you and what doesn't. When you've tried to communicate something and been misunderstood, ask yourself how you could approach the same situation differently next time. How can you become more functional? Viva la evolution. ☺

Chapter Three

IT STARTS WITH YOU

I stood there with the letter in my hand, enraged. I saw red. Literally. I was so completely angry, anything I saw around me was through a haze of hot-blood-red. And then I was storming, one furious foot after the other, directly and single-mindedly, from the post office where I'd collected the report card and dismissal letter toward the origin of the news, the National Institute of Dramatic Art. I hardly even remember this march. I remember the color red. I remember the rage of injustice. I didn't know that at the core of the emotion ravaging through me were the war cries of my ego, my sense of identity feeling utterly and unfairly attacked.

It must have taken an hour to walk there. I wasn't aware. Thoughts were racing through my head at breakneck speed. "You failed me in every subject?!! Every fuckin' subject?!! Music? How the fuck did you fail me in music? I helped the teacher teach the class!! I never got less than 98 percent for a fuckin' test!! *What the fuck!!!* I've been kicked out of NIDA! *Noooooooo!* This is my destiny! This is my life purpose!!" I was roaring like Mel Gibson's William Wallace from *Braveheart* in my head, and he was the one alumnus student whose framed headshot I looked at every time I passed it in the school corridors.

The walk must've done little to take the edge off my anger, for when I stormed through the school and barged into each classroom on a mission to confront the music teacher, I left a trail of terrified-looking summer students and rattled staff. I wasn't going down without a fight—or at least some retribution.

I did finally get to ask my music teacher the only question I had for her: "How did *you* fail *me* in music?" It was a few days later, in a meeting mediated by the head of the acting department. The one who had instructed all the other teachers to fail me in their classes. He tried to intervene. I told him to shut the fuck up. I asked her again. She sat there, shaking, in silence. I left and never looked back.

Twenty-one years old, with no idea really how the layers of this human experience interplay, I thought I was angry at Injustice and The System, when really, I was just taking the cut to the quick of my heart completely personally—the death of my dreams and more evidence for a subconscious, dysfunctional childhood belief: "I'm not good enough." I was hit for six so badly because I couldn't see any "bigger picture." The whole tragedy was happening deep in the guts of my intimacy, my vulnerability, my shame, and my fears. It felt like my life and death was on the line, when really it was just the next opportunity for me to either expand or contract along my way.

~~~

Imagine yourself in the center of a series of rings—concentric circles, one after the other, each circling wider and wider around the one before. The most intimate and inescapable relationship you have is there at the core: the relationship with your Self. In the next ring out are your most loved ones, your partner and children. The one after that, perhaps, has your parents and siblings. One ring farther out are your closest friends, and in the ring beyond that, maybe some work colleagues, or mates from a sporting team. Imagine the rings extending through and beyond all the levels of connection and relationship you have with others, right out to those you don't know and may never meet.

No matter which ring you are engaging with in any interaction, the experience and subsequent outcome will be determined by the quality of the communication. The closer the ring is to you—your center point—the trickier it can be to navigate the sea of emotions when the conversations are turbulent. Have you noticed how you can get way more triggered by family members, your partner, or even more so, your children? Interesting, huh?

So, there you are, at the center of the rings, right in the core of it all. Arguably the most important, subtle, and potentially profound relationship of them all: the one with self. How well do you communicate with You?

Which words do you commonly use? What is the quality of your self-talk like? When you make mistakes, are your words kind or cruel? When you see yourself naked in the mirror, what is that subtle, internal voice saying? For you, as a man, a lot of your self-judgement will consist of comparisons to the ideas you have of "what a man should be." Ask yourself where you got these ideas. Where did you learn them? Are they necessarily true?

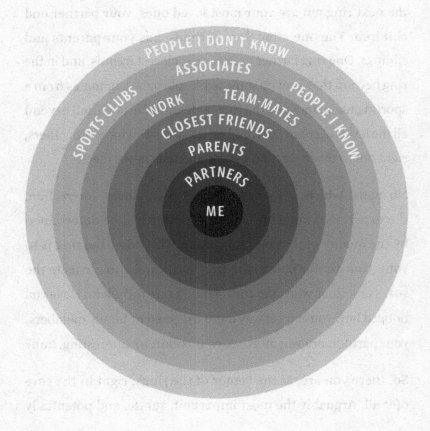

Your internal voice is constantly chattering away: justifying, consolidating, confabulating, chastising, rehearsing, or just plain rambling. The quality of this monologue then flavors your state of mind, how calm or turbulent your inner world is. The stormier your inner world is, the more interference there is between you and clear perception. It's harder for you to truly understand what you're feeling. It's certainly much harder to get a read on what others are feeling and communicating.

When you think about it, your whole experience of life, your version of reality, is experienced in your mind. All information from the environment is received through your senses in "bits," and then represented as a cohesive visual, auditory, and kinesthetic landscape projection in your mind. Now, this is all well and good, but it's important to know that we filter all data. We distort the information we receive; we delete a lot of it, and we fill in the gaps of missing information to construct a congruent internal picture. We do this "editing" of reality based on our beliefs and biases, based on our relationship with the past. This internal world is essentially a relationship-with-self. And your relationship-with-self determines the quality of your internal and external realities.

The less resolved you are with your past, the more distorted your interpretation of the present will be (and in each present moment, you are creating your future!). The less resolved you are with yourself, the more you are getting in the way of clarity in this moment—i.e., the harder it is to engage with clear communication.

The information you receive through sight, sound, smell, touch, and taste has to make its way through the complex filters of your belief systems. The more stories you are clinging to, especially if they involve unresolved anger, resent, shame, guilt, or regret, the thicker your lens of interference and distortion will be. It is harder to understand where others are actually coming from because your own spin on their communication is so thick.

———~———

I was gripped by pure fear. Six-year-old in fight or flight, with nowhere to run to, and yes, nowhere to hide. I had never seen Dad *so* angry. The look in his eyes scared the living shit out of me. He was storming over to where I had landed after throwing me across the room. He was intent on smacking me, grabbing me, and throwing me again in a fit of rage.

He had never lost it like this, and I don't remember him ever losing it this badly again. My recollection of the event is a memory of a memory. But I do know that it went down, and I made it mean something. The innocent little six-year-old can easily be forgiven for starting to believe he wasn't good enough. Enough to make the most important man happy. Enough for the man on the pedestal.

The fear of "not being enough" begins to become a belief. Sneakily, secretly, and silently embedding itself in the subconscious mind. And it starts: the second-guessing, the internal worry, the self-doubt. The self-perpetuating and self-fulfilling prophecy has commenced, and the flavor of that incessant, ever-present internal monologue has begun its overture.

~~~~~

When you are triggered by something in the present, it will usually be because of something you are unresolved with in the past. Someone says something and you react aggressively, or you feel yourself shut down and retreat. This is history repeating. Some of our past traumas exist in our minds'/bodies' (cellular memory) subconscious. This can make it super tricky to resolve, because we are not even aware of them. Triggers can also be very subtle. You and I could walk into the same room and have a very different intuitive experience because someone is wearing the same fragrance an abusive relative wore when you were a toddler. You may not even recognize the perfume, but you say to me, "I have a bad feeling in this room. I don't know why; I just feel uneasy." (For a technique to help heal subconscious trauma, see strategy number two at the end of this chapter.)

The practice of self-acceptance (past-acceptance) is such an important part of being able to see and hear others clearly. The more okay you are with yourself (i.e., your past), the more resolved you are, the less it's about you in communication and the more it can be about others and the communication itself—the more present in The Present you can be.

Our ego (see Chapter Four), which is simply our sense of identity, is very often defensive. The ego, being your understanding of *I* separate from others and all else, takes everything personally and is reactionary during communication. When ego gets in the way, it's hard for us to collaborate and allow our ideas to be challenged without feeling we're being personally attacked.

In relationships, when the ego gets in the way, it's hard to truly understand where our partner is coming from when they are expressing themselves, because the ego is too busy creating a defense strategy and preparing to justify itself. In our work, the part of us that jumps (a little desperately) to justifying, in the face of constructive feedback, is our ego. The more deeply confident and comfortable you are with self, the less need there is for the ego to defend.

Basically, the healthier your sense of identity (the better your relationship-with-self), the easier and more clearly you can see and communicate with others. This is one of the reasons I am such an advocate of personal development and self-acceptance. Improving your Conscious Comms with others starts by getting good with *you*.

Strategies to Improve Your Relationship-With-Self

SELF-ACCEPTANCE

You are exactly as you should be in this moment, right here, right now, just the way you are. How do I know this? Because reality told me. There you are. Just like that, with all your bits and bobs. So, apparently, you are exactly as you are supposed to be in this moment. Perfectly imperfect and completely good enough to be you. You shouldn't be more like anyone else, because you're not anyone else! You are doing a perfect job being you. As one of my favorite authors/thinkers, Byron Katie, says, "You can argue with reality, but reality will win...only 100 percent of the time!"

By the way, this doesn't mean you might not want to continue to improve as time passes and you project into your future, to get better at being you. It just means that, in the snapshot of this moment, you are exactly as you are supposed to be. This is about complete acceptance of the past and present moment, and of yourself.

When you can accept and even love all that you've been and are (yes, even the stuff you regret), your relationship-with-self moves from toxic to resolved. When you are resolved with self, you've freed up mind space to be more present, to communicate more clearly with life and with others. You can better "see" with less interference and past "baggage." You also have more mind capacity for others.

Here is a tool to help you with accepting the past: CIA (no, not the Central Intelligence Agency!). This acronym was developed by Neil and Sue Thompson in their 2008 book *The Critically Reflective Practitioner*. It is one of the most helpful and regularly used tools I've adopted. "Control, Influence, Accept." There are some things in life you can control. If something is within your control and it's not the way you would like it to be, rock on, give it all your energy. Give it all your worry, concern, attention, and your blood, sweat, and tears, to make it better. Then there are some things that are not in your control, but that you have some influence over. Great. Give them the appropriate amount of your energy; the appropriate amount of your sleepless night figuring out a solution. If you only have 1 percent influence, then give only 1 percent concern. 80 percent influence? 80 percent concern. Then there are things you can't control or influence, and they go straight into the "accept" basket. Zero worry. Zero stress. Zero frustration, and none of your sleepless-night distractions!

Here is some more gold from CIA. *Everything* from your past can go straight into the accept basket! Why? Because it all qualifies as things you can't control or influence. Apparently, it all should have happened. Why? Because it did. This includes every action you took that you hope you won't take again. Viva la improvement![3]*

ACKNOWLEDGE/GRATITUDE/LET GO

I came across this healing process in a book called *The Untethered Soul* by Michael Singer. The technique is beautifully simple and subtle, and I've been finding it very helpful. Quite simply, when you are triggered by something, the first step is to express gratitude for being triggered. Why? Well, because when something triggers you and you get upset in that moment, the past trauma has gone from being dormant in your subconscious to being active in your conscious awareness. Only when you are conscious of something can you then let it go. You can't let go of something when you are not aware of it! Note: You don't even need to be aware of exactly what the trauma was. You just need to notice that something triggered you and you reacted.

The next step is to let it go.

You may be asking, How do I do that? How do I "let it go"? There is no prescription for this. You get to make up a way that works for you. Language is powerful, so it will certainly help you to use words. Saying something like, "I am grateful for being triggered

---

3 * It is important to note here that using CIA as a tool is like any other practice; you need to keep doing it. Quite often you will put something in the accept basket and, at some point, it creeps back out and you catch yourself stressing about it again. That's okay—just put it back in the accept basket and carry on. Like any practice, with repetition, you get better at it. Over time, you will notice less rumination over things you've previously accepted.

right now. Thank you. Now I practice nonattachment to the past, and I let that trauma go." Another way to let go is through your body. As you speak your words of release, let your shoulders drop. Be aware of relaxing any places of tension in your body. Take some deeper breaths and exhale with a sense of letting go. Combining language and physical release works well.

Of course, doing this once won't necessarily heal your neural and/or cellular echoes of the past. This also is a practice, and you need to keep doing it. The more traumatic the event was in the past, the longer it may take you to smooth out the creases, so to speak. Like any practice that's good for you—meditation, yoga, Pilates, etc.—you don't just get good at it, tick the box, and then stop. It's something you keep doing. (Are you noticing a theme yet? The strategies I'm sharing in this book need to become habitual practices.)

SELF-TALK

Start to notice and become more aware of the words and tone you use in your head when you are alone. When it's negative, change it. Another practice: Be persistently kind in the way you talk to yourself. You will find over time that your default tone-to-self changes and it becomes more habitual to talk to yourself in a positive, supportive, and loving way.

This doesn't mean not to hold yourself accountable to trying to be the best version of you. It just means, when you slip (and we do that, we humans), pick yourself up and encourage yourself to get back on your game, in a kind way. There is never a reason to be cruel. Cruelty is simply dysfunctional.

It's crazy when you think about it. We are prone to speak way more harshly to ourselves than we ever would to anyone else. Why is that? Do we like others more than we like ourselves? How can that be? We are all equal, aren't we? Are you not as deserving of love as your child or sister or friend? Speak kindly to yourself. Ease up on your imperfections and focus on your intentions. If your intentions are good, you're good.

SELF-CARE

What are the things you know are good for your well-being that you don't do? What are the excuses you've been using for not rejuvenating and replenishing? Are you someone who has tipped the balance toward helping everyone else, to your own detriment? Perhaps you've buried yourself in your work. Maybe you've bought into the belief that "there's not enough time for me." Maybe you deal with overwhelm by procrastinating. And, when you do invest time in yourself, do you do it guilt-free?

If it makes it easier to get your head around doing good things for yourself, look at it like this: you can only give/serve/contribute/help others if you have the energy reserves and clarity to do so. If you want to keep making it about everyone else, you have to look after you. And remember, by getting good with you, you can more easily get out of the way for clearer and more connected communication.

WHAT ARE THE THINGS YOU CAN DO THAT ARE GOOD FOR YOU?

Here is a strategy to make sure you actually do them. This quadrant model comes from a book by the late Stephen Covey called *The 7 Habits of Highly Effective People*. He called the seventh habit "sharpening the saw." By this he meant, if you are always using the saw (yourself) without taking time to look after it and keep it in good condition, it will go blunt and your ability to cut wood will diminish.

The following diagram is a time-management matrix described and depicted in Stephen Covey's work.

Quadrants 1 and 2 both contain the things to do that are important. Quadrants 3 and 4 are things that are not important. Quadrants 1 and 3 are urgent, and 2 and 4 are not urgent.

Q2 is shaded because this is an effective space to spend time in. The more time you spend in Q2, the fewer things will show up in Q1 and Q3. However, without a conscious strategy to spend time in Q2, we end up spending most of our time over in Q1 and Q3.

So here is the simple strategy: schedule time for Q2. Get your calendar and choose a block of time as a repeating weekly event for Q2. Make your self-care a priority in this time. Once it's in the calendar, you are more likely to schedule other matters around it and actually dedicate time to it.

IMPORTANT

	QUADRANT 1	**QUADRANT 2**	
URGENT	• crisis • emergency meetings • last-minute deadlines • pressing problems • spot fires • unforeseen events	• nurturing relationships • long-term goal setting • personal resilience activities • strategy and big-picture design • planning and prevention • recreation • learning and personal growth	**NOT URGENT**
	QUADRANT 3 • needless interruptions • unnecessary reports • irrelevant meetings • below the line issues • unimportant emails, phone calls, tasks, status updates, ect.	**QUADRANT 1** • avoidanc activities • excessive TV, gaming, social media scrolling • time wasters • gossip • etc.	

NOT IMPORTANT

Chapter Four

IDENTITY

The London winter of 1997 was descending upon the city—cold, wet, and forbidding. I was lost. I was alone. I was as far from home as possible. The recreational use of substances was creeping from the weekends and further into the weekdays, and for the first time in my life, at the ripe age of twenty-six, I had experienced heartbreak—properly painful, torturous, and very teary. My teenage sweetheart and betrothed had finally mustered the courage to do what had to be done and neither of us had known how to do. She ended the relationship. She packed up her belongings, and our flatmates helped her move to the apartment of another man—someone she had recently met. I was broken. For reasons not then understood by me, our small group of friends felt they needed to take a side: hers. Great! All alone at Heartbreak Hotel and no one to drown my sorrows with!

Dark days indeed. I drowned them alone, nonetheless.

In the years leading up to this pivotal period, I had been searching for identity, trying to etch out a persona by rebelling against everything mainstream. My version of punk had me collecting tattoos and facial piercings, and cultivating multi-colored dreadlocks. I was trying to be someone, trying to say something, but no one really understood. I had got to a point of no direction. After two turbulent years of being in and out of the relationship, my final turnaround devotion to her was part of my undoing. "You're all that matters to me, baby. I just want to be with you." I had no mission. I had no plan.

She confessed to me, "You just don't feel like a man. It's hard to explain, Jem. When we have sex, there's no spark. I don't feel like you're taking me anywhere. The attraction's gone. It just doesn't feel right. I'm sorry."

Punch to the gut. Urggghhh. Confusion amidst the grief. What does she mean I'm not a man? I'm a twenty-six-year-old male. How can I *not* be a man?! What else do I need to do? This was the boy/man riddle I didn't begin to find answers to until several years later, and then kept learning for decades after.

As my world came crumbling down around me, I started to develop a stutter. I noticed more and more people having to ask me to repeat myself because they didn't hear what I had said. I was retreating to an inner world of self-doubt and deprecation. I had even forgotten the reason for being in London this time round: to save up enough money to get back to India and spend a year barefoot and free. My ability to communicate was quickly eroding, and isolation in a city of millions became very real.

Then an angel appeared. My sister was living and working around Europe and the UK at the time. She came to visit me and reminded me who, where, and why I was. "I'll be in India in December," she said. "Come and meet me in Varanasi." I bought my ticket that week.

What ensued was the first of two times in my life when I experienced, to some degree, the death of ego: an identity crisis/opportunity, the chance to start from scratch and consciously repair my relationship-with-self.

I began by dropping my attachment to all the "vehicles" I had previously identified with that were no longer there. I was no longer "her partner." I was no longer an actor, motorcycle courier, bartender, laborer, or punk. I didn't have to be anyone or do anything. I decided to run an experiment of letting go of any design on the future. I literally moved day-to-day as I felt, and hence ended up experiencing a year of remarkable and magical flow, free from the constraints of who I thought I should be.

Unfortunately for my parents, my need to break ties meant that communication with anyone not in my immediate and present situation became almost nonexistent. I was relatively off the grid. I even got to the point of following the dry-season weather so that I could live predominantly outdoors—sleeping in a hammock, cooking meals on a fire, and getting water from local springs.

Mum and Dad would go many months at a time without any correspondence. This was back in the days before email was normal (does anyone remember that time?) and any snail mail went to a city's Poste Restante. You can imagine a lot of the letters meant for me went unread and unanswered. On reflection, I feel bad for them—not knowing where their eldest child was, if he was safe, if he was okay.

This year of separation from the past, of reidentification, reconnection to self and then others, was also a year of relearning how to communicate. Learning how to listen lightly to the more subtle tones. Learning how to speak more gently to myself in those internal conversations. Learning the basic building blocks of a foreign language, and how to get by in the world with very few words. This year was me learning better ways to communicate more consciously with Life.

Ego in Communication

Twenty-two years later. October 2019. We had reached the spot to make camp for the night, about 4,500 meters elevation, above the tree line. Finding firewood was going to be a mission. A mountain stream ran beside the camp, so at least fresh water was easy. It had been a big day of trekking. Our clients and the packhorses alike were exhausted. We had about twenty minutes of sunlight before our primary source of warmth would descend behind one of the majestic Himalayan peaks surrounding us. It was about to get very cold.

I scoped the site for a flat and smooth patch of grass to pitch our tent. I was feeling good and "in my manhood," building shelter for my woman. *Ugg. Me man. Me make shelter.* I found a spot on top of a grassy knoll next to the stream. The clients, who had come from Australia to join our Himalayan Experience Leadership Program, were all getting busy pitching their tents too.

Then my partner walked up and gently suggested, "Baby, wouldn't we be more sheltered from the wind down there?" as she pointed to a different potential location. I didn't want to set up down there because the ground was lumpy, and it would mean more work with a hatchet to level it. "I think here will be fine," I replied.

She left it at that and went over to help set up the camp kitchen tent with our local Himachali mountain brothers. I thought about it, then decided to move the tent to where she had suggested. I was silently grumpy while flattening the earth. After getting the tent up and the sleeping mats and bags sorted, I walked over to the fire they had made and were sitting around, and I asked our brother and guide, Pappu, if he thought it would've become too windy and unprotected up on the plot I had originally set up at. He confirmed my partner's intuition. "*Hun ji.* Yes, *bhai.* It would not be good to camp up there." I felt stupid. I felt dumb. I cracked the shits and had a little tantrum. "Yeah, fine, you were right! I'm just trying to look after you," my bruised ego blurted out.

I about-faced and walked off toward the tent, initially to sulk momentarily, and then to take a deep breath, and have a little chat with my ego. "Oh ego, look at you go! Getting all upset because you looked silly. It's okay, mate. Everything's alright. We are not in danger! It's okay to make mistakes," I said to myself as I looked up at the first stars beginning to appear in the darkening sky. Breathe, release, let go, and return to my place of equanimity.

By the time she came over to me a few minutes later, to hug me and kiss me, look in my eyes and tell me she loved me, I had already moved beyond my ego to let it dissipate into distant whispers and then silence. I was ready for immediate and complete reconnection.

In the years before understanding what I'm about to share with you in this chapter, it would have taken *much* longer to move on. And there's a good chance there would have been a tiny splinter of resentment still wedged in me somewhere, to aggravate and accumulate into the future version of "me" and the relationship!

~~~

We all have one, an ego. It's part of being human. Our ego serves a purpose and, despite what many spiritual books might say, ego is not categorically "bad." In fact, I believe we can develop a healthy and functional ego. However, left unchecked, our ego will assume the driver's seat of our bus, to its own end. And this end is not necessarily to serve the greater good of the communication process! You may have noticed (usually retrospectively) that there've been many times when you reacted emotionally to a trigger in a conversation and completely derailed the train of communication. Our ego is essentially "me-centric" and very defensive, so therefore mainly not interested in serving the greater good of the comms.

The most effective way to prevent this "rogue controller" is simply with awareness.

My intention in this chapter is not to explain the intricacies or machinations of the ego deeply or completely as understood by the great philosophers and psychologists. What I hope to do is give a simplified definition and point out some easy-to-recognize traits of the ego, to help you become more easily aware. I will also talk about how and when ego can get in the way of successful communication, when it can also play a functional role, and how becoming more conscious in comms can help us navigate the challenges our egos present.

Our ego is simply our sense of identity—who you think you are. Our ego defines itself in being separate from others and its surroundings. Some basics to point out: it's an illusion, a made-up thing that exists only in our thoughts. We weren't born with an ego. Those of you with children will remember when a brand-new baby is born; they don't come out with a formed sense of identity. For bubs, it's all just lights and sounds and sensations.

Then, over those formative years, through a combination of nurture, nature, and meaning-making, the remarkable process of an emerging personality (ego formation) takes place right in front of the parents' eyes.

Your ego would have you believe it's the origin of you, that it came first. But having an ego is a result of having a brain/mind, not the other way around. It also would convince you that the death of ego (an identity crisis) is akin to real, actual death. But it's not. An identity crisis can actually present as an opportunity to reidentify (hopefully with some positive modifications!). The London-to-India story I shared at the start of this chapter was the first of two times I have experienced this identity crisis/opportunity. Decades later, in my early forties, I was lucky enough to go through the process again, that time with more awareness, more consciously, and with a clearer intention to improve my relationship-with-self. Update and upgrade the software, so to speak.

It is said that, through our evolution, the ego developed as a protection mechanism—to keep us safe. It is therefore fueled by fear, and extremely defensive. In fact, we tend to defend our sense of identity above all else. This explains why we get terribly reactive when we feel like our character is in question. Interestingly, neuroscientists using fMRI (a way to measure brain activity) have noticed that, whether we talk about our ideologies and political opinions or whether we talk about our sense of identity, the same part of the brain lights up. This suggests we identify closely with those beliefs in particular, and accordingly become emotional when they are challenged.

To help you get better at catching your ego before it has its own way, here are six common traits to become aware of. They are listed here in no particular order. They sometimes serve a functional purpose, but they are also often only self-serving, and can sabotage rational conversations before you know what's happened!

1. THE NEED TO JUDGE

When you notice yourself judging others (or even yourself), you guessed it, that's your ego. It needs to do this to reinforce its sense of identity. When you hear that voice in your head making a negative, passing judgement of another person, it's not usually about them. It's your ego saying, *I would never wear that awful jacket*, or *I would never treat my children like that*. For the ego, it's all in reference to self. Similarly, in positive judgement, you might be looking at a stranger and thinking, *I reckon that's a nice person. I like their jeans. Oh, and they seem very polite*. What your ego is really saying is, *I'd wear those jeans. I think I'm polite*.

When you're driving in traffic and you make space for a merging car to come in front of you, and the other driver doesn't give you that little thank-you hand-wave, the voice in your head (or perhaps that even gets vocalized) says, "What a rude asshole!" Yep, hello again, ego!

These moments of judgement can get in the way of potential communication because they can narrow your scope of open-mindedness and curiosity. Because of your prejudgment of others and/or situations, you already have preconceived ideas of any forthcoming communication. You are less likely to truly hear or understand clearly what others are trying to say.

2. THE NEED TO JUSTIFY

You know that tone of your voice when someone questions you, or asks why you did something? That slightly defensive and perhaps even desperate tone when you justify your actions? Yes, fellas, that's just your ego. When your boss passes by your desk and asks if you've finished the report, and before you know it you've reacted with excuses, yep, you guessed it—your ego got in first again.

There are many times when people miss the point because they are either internally or outwardly jumping to justify and defend their perspective, their ideas, their way of doing things—their identity.

I remember a particular evening in my marriage, in a time when I wasn't awake to when my ego was in control. My wife arrived home after work on a day in our routine when I was home with the kids. Normally on this day, by the time she got home, dinner was cooked, and the kitchen was clean. This particular night, it wasn't. Her simple observation, "Oh, the kitchen's not done," could have been taken as such, but ohhhh no, my ego heard that as a personal attack! Quick, launch into defensive justification, with a slightly aggressive tone and one notch up on the volume control!

"Well, the kids had this thing after school you didn't tell me about, and then we had a flat tire on the way home, and then there was no milk in the fridge, and I had to turn around and go back to the shops! I've actually had a really shit day, and then you walk in and criticize me for not doing the bloody kitchen on time!"

Gee whiz, ego, anyone would think it was a matter of life and death, given the desperation of your justification! Hilarious. I reflect now and wonder how that conversation (and *so* many others like it) would've played out if I'd simply replied, "No, not yet. I'll get to it. Hi love, how was your day?"

3. THE NEED TO LOOK GOOD

Our ego hates looking stupid (yep, that certainly was my ego spitting the dummy after setting up our tent in the Himalayas!). When you trip over yourself publicly and feel like a fool, wishing the ground would swallow you up, that's just your ego. When you pretend to know more than you do in a conversation, making up some fact or statistic, it's your ego needing to look good.

When you're working in a team situation, perhaps collaborating or workshopping to create solutions, the part of you that doesn't want to speak up and share your "crazy idea" for fear of looking stupid is your ego. Imagine how many genius ideas have been left unsaid because of ego!

When you do share an idea and someone challenges it, your ego takes it personally, perceives the challenge as a threat, and shuts down the potentially collaborative communication. If this has been a consistent pattern for you, there is a good chance people just stop trying to work with you (hello disconnection/isolation).

4. THE NEED TO BE RIGHT

Everything was perfect. Honeymoon-esque. Warm sun setting over the Balinese ocean. The two of us side by side, cocktails in hand, reclined on the poolside lounges, food in our bellies, and not a care in the world. Bathing in our burgeoning love. All four kids back home in Australia. Perfect.

A familiar song plays on the sound system.

"Oh," my love comments, "this song's off [album]."

I'm sure it's not.

"I don't think it is…" I reply.

"Yeah, I'm pretty sure it is."

"Oh, okay."

Pause…internal observation…

Ego fires up in my mind. "Tell her it's not. She needs to know she's wrong. You can't let her go on thinking the wrong thing. Go on, get out your phone and Google it. You can show her pretty quickly you're right!" and so on.

Internal voice of awareness arrives: "Hi, ego. I see you. Bless your cotton socks! Look at you go, desperate to be right. It's okay. We are not in danger right now. Everything is alright." With the light switched on and the ego seen, it very quickly dissipates.

Resume the ambience. As you were. Love vibes unruffled. Happiness. Undisturbed bliss. Cocktail-sipping and sunset-gazing. Ahhhhh.

If I had let my ego have its way, we would have disagreed, and perhaps got out our phones to see who was right. One of us would've "won." But that perfect, beautiful energy that we were enjoying would have then had a little glitch in it, a subtle tone of disharmony. Better to just let it be. And let our divine little bubble together continue on glitch-free.

~~~~

Have you ever said to someone, "I told you so," when it turned out that you were right? Or perhaps you've even just thought to yourself, *I knew it all along!* Have you ever been in arguments with a friend or partner over things that don't really matter? Perhaps you both seek resolution with a Google war to settle the matter. Our egos don't mind creating conflict if it means being right.

Sometimes this need to be right can serve a purpose. For example, imagine if the team meeting time had been changed and one of your teammates missed the email. You are disagreeing on the meeting time, you know you're right, and you will prove it to them because you don't want them showing up at the wrong time. Functional.

But so often, it's not important and doesn't really matter. How would the relationship be if you just let it slide? What would (or wouldn't) happen if you just let the other person keep believing that it was November five years ago, not October, that you last went camping together? Does it really matter? Is it worth arguing over or proving them wrong?

A question worth asking yourself before going to a right-or-wrong war is, "For what purpose? If I choose to argue this point right now, why am doing it?"

5. THE NEED TO KNOW

Imagine this: you're walking past the kitchen, and you overhear your partner and a friend talking about you. At the very least, your ears prick up as you pause at the door, straining to hear what they are saying about you. Maybe you just walk right in, interrupt, and ask what they are saying. When they reply, "We are talking about you, not to you," your ego fires up even more, wanting to know what they are saying.

Remember a time when you were in the same room and a friend was scrolling through a social media feed, came across something funny, and laughed out loud. The part of you that says, "What? What are you laughing at?" is just your ego. They might reply with, "Oh, it's nothing," and now your ego wants to know even more! Again, the question "For what purpose?" could serve you well in this situation. Perhaps the reason is just to engage in some light banter and cultivate the connection between you. Good enough reason, then, in that case, to carry on with your ego's need to know what they're laughing at.

6. THE NEED TO GET EVEN

This need always takes me back to the playground in school. One of your friends plays a trick on you, and you spend the next week scheming how to get them back. Your ego is consumed until payback time! Actually, for me, being smaller and more shy than other kids, I was less likely to take payback action because of the fear of even fiercer retribution, so I would let it slide and just feel resentment instead!

Even when people say, "Karma will get you," they might not want to exact the punishment themselves, but the part of them that hopes something will happen to a person, to pay them back, is just their ego.

Once again, this need to get even can sometimes be just fine. Take, for example, competitive sport. Imagine the last time two tennis players competed and one of them was beaten. The next time they meet, the loser's determination to win and get even makes for a great tennis match—no harm there.

Working with Ego

It's a good idea not to go to war on your ego. If you try to control it or "make it go away," you will essentially fuel its fire by fighting with it. The war on drugs? More drugs. The war on poverty? More poverty. The war on terror? More terrorism.

It also very rarely works to call someone else out on their ego. This usually tends to fire things up, unless you have asked each other for help noticing when your ego is driving, for your own self-development. Even then, you will notice how uncomfortable it is to be called out on your ego.

I find the most effective way to not be controlled by your ego is to simply notice it. Just shine the light on it. By having awareness that it's your ego carrying on in any given moment, and letting it be without taking the action it wants, the ego intensity seems to dissipate. I sometimes even call it out with love. *Hey ego, look at you go, desperate to _____ (be right, e.g.). It's okay, we are safe right now, our life is not in danger. Carry on as a voice in my head, but I've got your number, I know it's you.*

When I do this lightheartedly, knowingly and lovingly, the ego part of me becomes quieter, and an internal space of potential expands.

The better we get at being aware of our ego before it takes over, creating a moment to pause and become more conscious, the better we can be in our role in the communication process. The ability to pause before reacting creates more options for how we choose to respond. We literally are improving our response-ability! We become more responsible as conscious communicators.

Chapter Five

MEN, EMOTIONS, AND COMMUNICATION

My sons and I love a good game of footy. For those of you reading this outside of Australia, the code we follow is called AFL (Australian Football League). When you understand how it works, it's an awesome spectacle: fast, exhilarating, and super skillful.

In 2017, we were gathered at a house in the small town where my sister and her family live to watch the season Grand Final. We had only met our hosts and the other guests for the first time that day, but the scene was completely familiar. The smell of assorted meats sizzling away on the BBQ, crackers, dips, and salads on a trestle table, cold drinks in a cooler full of ice, boisterous and slightly drunken supporting and banter.

The victors of the day had been an underdog team for decades, Richmond Tigers. They triumphed for the first time in thirty-seven years. For their players, coaches, and supporters, it was an emotional day. My boys and I were sitting together, front row, enjoying the theatre of celebrations post-game. One famous ex-player and club devotee was there on screen, unashamedly, with tears streaming down his face. From behind us came the heckle, "Hahaha... Ahhhhhhh, stop crying, you stupid pussy, what a bloody wimp!"

Both of my boys, thirteen and eleven years old at the time, turned around in unison and retorted quite earnestly, "What's wrong with men crying?" The tone in their voices suggested the fella behind us was out of line and had something wrong with him. He had no reply, other than to pipe down and take another slug on his beer. Truth and wisdom from the mouths of children!

Insert proud dad moment here.

My younger boy once said, whilst walking next to me holding my hand, "Dad, I think I understand why tears are healthy. Because you are feeling a strong emotion inside you, and the tears can carry it out of your body." He said this to me on the anniversary of my brother's death, as we were walking away from the shrine and the tears were rolling over my cheeks.

Men do have access to the full range of emotions. Men are human. Humans have emotions. That's just the bottom line. Perhaps you are a man who knows this. Or maybe you've been told you can't access your emotions and you can't communicate well. Either way, further contemplation and practice of tuning in to what you are feeling, and then sharing that with someone who cares, is healthy.

Some people are naturally more kinesthetic (feeling) in their approach to life, while others are naturally more auditory-digital, which is a term to describe the representational system of logic and the way we talk to ourselves. Then there are those people who are more visual in their processing. Of course, we can be a blend of all three and move between them. If you are someone who is naturally more "in your head" (auditory-digital), then the question, "How do you feel about that?" may come across as slightly strange to you. You might not "feel" anything at all. For you, it may be more about whether something makes sense or not.

Regardless of your natural processing modality, taking mindful moments to pause and turn your attention inward can be helpful. Using language to help create some clarity on "where you are at" is a powerful tool, and obviously necessary if you then want to communicate how you feel to someone else.

You can't get this process wrong, it's completely personal and subjective. If you sit quietly, inquire within, and simply say, "I feel..." then see what comes to you. Whatever it is you say is what it is for you. It's your state of being in each moment, so you can call it what you like. If you're feeling neutral (nondescript, nothing in particular), give it a word. "I am feeling calm." Or, "tranquil," or "settled." The more you practice this inward attention, the more attuned you will get to the more subtle emotional flavors of your state. Sometimes you may have initially thought you weren't feeling anything, then, when you become quiet and curious, you might detect a hint of something. Is there an agitation or restlessness? Maybe you can notice some kind of reaction to the process itself. Say the sentence, "I feel _____" [insert your word].

Obviously, there are times at the opposite end of the feeling scale, when the emotions are magnified and perhaps even overwhelming. This too is a good time to put it into words. "I'm feeling really [angry] right now!" or whatever it is for you in that moment.

Sometimes you might notice internal sensations and you're not even sure what the emotion is. Notice the sensations themselves as physical manifestations. You could say, "I feel a bit weird right now. I'm not sure what it is. I feel a jittery sensation in my chest." Or, "I feel my heart rate accelerated." Or, "I feel a heat sensation in my head," etc. You don't need to try and change what you are feeling. Just simply notice it and give it some words.

The next step in this process is an exercise in vulnerability. Share, with someone who cares, what or how you are feeling. Despite what you may have been taught by society or culture, vulnerability is a strength. When you have the courage to admit your vulnerability, you are allowing yourself to be more accessible to others. People can connect with you more deeply, because they relate. "Oh wow, he's like me. I'm not alone. I know how he feels."

We are all vulnerable. Your life will end (definitely) *and* you have no idea when! You could get sick or have an accident that's completely out of your control. I don't say this to be morbid or invoke fear, I say this because it's reality and it's something we all have in common. The COVID-19 pandemic has been (and still is at the time of writing this) a massive in-your-face reminder of how vulnerable we all are. Our vulnerability is a connector between us, and as mentioned in previous chapters, we survive and thrive as a collective, not on our own.

As well as developing the inclination to share more often how you are feeling, you could also make the effort to reach out to other men and ask them how they are doing, especially if you think someone you know might be going through something. Maybe they are not as jovial as usual, or maybe they are more quiet than normal. Creating the opportunity for them to express how they are feeling will often be very welcomed.

An Empowering Tip

When you are communicating how you feel, either to yourself or someone else, don't give your power away. If you were to say, "You make me feel so [frustrated] when you _____" then you are telling yourself (and the other person) that they have some control over how you feel. That way, you are a victim and at the mercy of others. It's better for you to word it something like this: "When you _____, I feel [frustrated]." This way, you are owning your emotional reaction to situations, which means the power to process the feeling and be the "driver of your own bus," so to speak, is with you and not the other person.

You can still communicate how you feel, whilst maintaining responsibility for your feelings. Once again, this slight framing adjustment improves your response-ability.

Getting Stuck

I would like to return here to the concentric circles I mentioned earlier in Chapter Three. It would seem that there are some common factors that can contribute to us "choking up" in communication. From a combination of self-observation and many thousands of hours coaching individuals, I've come to the understanding that the closer we are to the person communicating with us, and/or the closer to our sense of identity the topic is, the more susceptible we are to going blank, freezing, shutting down, or choking up.

It became such a familiar and always unpleasant feeling in my marriage when I would be triggered, get clouded in my head, and then not even be able to string a coherent sentence together. There I would be, feeling a wash of emotions while trying to explain myself, only to sound (and feel) like a fool. My wife used to tell me how terrible I was at communicating—understandably so, as in that context it was the truth. The strange thing was that at work, as a senior leader, I was known for being a wonderful communicator (operating with different levels of the concentric rings). Because my wife never saw that side of me, she found it hard to believe.

The closer someone is to us, the more likely we are to let our buttons be pushed by them.

However, there have been times when I wasn't so close to the people I was communicating with, but I've still frozen. There were times when I had to talk about myself. This is when the subject matter is right at the core of the rings, and that equals vulnerability.

One time, after being promoted to a regional manager role in the last company I worked for, I experienced an on-the-spot panic attack. We were at my first leaders' meeting with the state manager I would now report to. All we had to do was introduce ourselves and tell a little bit of our success story and how we came to be there in that role. When I started to speak, I froze so completely that the person next to me put her hand on my arm to comfort me and said, "It's okay. I'll go now. We can come back to you."

I didn't know the people very well (a few rings away), but the topic I had to talk about was right in the center: me and my success. Back then, I was still running a common (usually subconscious) human belief—"I'm not good enough." Choke.

This got me thinking. Are there times when you can be triggered emotionally by someone from a distant concentric ring? Someone you hardly know, let alone care about? And the answer is "yes," if the content is personal. This doesn't mean it necessarily happens every time. For me, it was a little less predictable. However, since devoting time to self-development and mindfulness practices, it seems to not happen much at all anymore. I still sometimes feel nerves and adrenaline when I speak at events, especially if talking about myself—just no more choking!

As I've said a few times now, with anything we do, the more we do it, the easier it gets. To begin with, communicating your emotions may require deep breaths and a big glass of water to lubricate that drying mouth! But after some time, it can become natural for you.

Perhaps you could even pause reading now for a moment, check in with how you feel, and put it into words. If there is anyone within earshot, maybe you could declare, "Excuse me, I just wanted to let you know I'm currently feeling _____" [emotion].

Part II

COMMS BEYOND YOU

Chapter Six

A WHOLE LOT MORE GOING ON

You might not believe the story I'm about to tell you. I don't blame you; it defies our understanding of what's physically and scientifically possible. But I was there, and it happened, and it showed me there's a whole realm of stuff we don't know, phenomena beyond our comprehension and current scientific ability to explain.

Early evening, balmy Koh San Road, Bangkok, year 2000: internet cafes, street markets, stripper bars, and drunk Western backpackers. It was our honeymoon, but not our first Asian rodeo. My newlywed wife and I were deep inside a small busy restaurant, enjoying green curry and watching a movie on a flickering TV screen hanging off the corner wall.

The Indian street performer who had been busking outside before he packed up his show walked through the restaurant and came directly to our table. "*Namaste*, sir," he said, as he smiled to me and bowed. He had our attention, and quickly the growing attention of the waiting staff and other travelers around us.

He then proceeded to take a twenty-baht note (Thai currency) out of his pocket and hand it to me. "Please sir, inspect the note." Sensing some illusion or trickery was about to be displayed, I did as he asked. Not just flippantly. Completely. When I was satisfied it was an ordinary note, with nothing attached, I handed it back to him. He was right there, close enough for me to smell the incense in the fabric of his clothes. Our performer took the note from my hand, held it about five inches above the table, placed his other hand about five inches above the note, and then let it go, leaving it to hover in midair.

"Please, sir, inspect the note," he said again. Now I was even more alert. I studied physics and math in high school. I had devoured books on quantum physics through my twenties. I was curious and analytical. I was also as straight as a die; no Thai weed had been smoked by me that day! I checked this hovering note with both hands, around and around, over and over, until I knew conclusively there was *nothing* attached to it. There it was. Hovering. Right in front of us.

Once he saw that I knew it was real, he took it out of the air, folded it, put it back in his top pocket, made a namaste with his hands, bowed slightly, smiled modestly, and left the restaurant. He didn't ask for anything. My wife and I looked at each other, speechless, and went back to our curry and movie. When the film was over, the first thing she said was, "Why did he choose us?" to which I replied, "Because we were ready for that information."

To this day, that bizarre experience means one thing to me; there is a lot of stuff going on that we don't know about and can't understand. The realms of possibility are beyond our comprehension and intuition. What actually happened in that little Koh San Road restaurant isn't the point. The point is, I couldn't explain it (I still can't), and that has to open the doors of Possibility and pose questions to Perception. As the philosopher Henry Thoreau once said, "It's not what you're looking at that matters, it's what you see."

A Spiritual Aspect to Communication

I want to be careful in communicating what I'm about to go into in this chapter—the potential spiritual aspect available in and for communication. As soon as the word "spiritual" is used, people's minds flood with connotations and predisposed ideas due to their beliefs and biases, values, and opinions. Whatever the word "spiritual" evokes for you, you certainly have your own take on it.

My take on it for the purpose of this book is, "That which is beyond ego, nonphysical, in its essence inexplicable, and experienced in the interconnectedness of everything."

I'm only somewhat curious as to what the "actual truth" is behind the mechanics of the universe. I do find it fascinating, but not ultimately important. After all, we can only ever know how the universe works from inside the human experience; therefore, we can never know the absolute truth, the workings of everything, completely objectively.

I am interested in (and keep reading and listening to) what science uncovers, but whether we can explain something or not doesn't determine our experience of it. I don't know how a video from my iPhone is AirDropped to my laptop in a few seconds, but that doesn't create an aversion to utilizing the technology. "Not knowing how" doesn't make the experience of using it anything other than convenient (or frustrating when it doesn't work!).

Beyond what we don't know, there's even a lot of stuff that we don't know we don't know. This is exciting. In Hindi they say "*Sab kuch milega,*" which means "Everything is possible." My belief is that anything within the laws of the universe is possible, and we don't know all the fundamental laws, so there is more possible than we can comprehend.

Phenomena we can experience, but not explain, are called mystical. Which phenomena fall into this category keeps changing as our ability to scientifically understand and explain continues to expand. Many things that were once mystical ow are not. For me, "spiritual" has a different element to it, a slightly more awe-inspiring aspect. A sense that we are all equally connected to each other and everything in a much grander and more beautiful way than we can imagine. We may never be able to scientifically explain it, but we can catch glimpses of it through our experiences.

When we don't have answers, when we can't prove or truly know how something works, we rely on our beliefs and intuitions. It's worth noting that both are often off the mark from what's actually occurring, and this doesn't necessarily matter. Both intuitions and beliefs can either serve us well or send us on unhelpful goose chases. A lot of our beliefs and intuitions we can't adequately explain (although we are very adept at justifying them to ourselves and others). We can, however, amend or adjust them, modify them to align with new information, or simply scrap them altogether. They need not (and perhaps should not) be fixed.

We believed the earth was flat (I find it fascinating that some people still do!), until we found out it isn't.

What's more important to me than explanations are these questions: how does any particular belief affect my well-being? How does it impact the way I treat others? Are there practical applications or practices I can derive from a belief that are functional or beneficial? Does it make enough sense to me and fit within my "map of reality?" I find it important, with any belief, to loosen my grip on it and be open to new perspectives and information that may challenge my existing ideas.

Spirituality is based on beliefs derived from tangible yet inexplicable experiences—one of which is the experience of being an intrinsic part of a much bigger field of existence. Language can only ever fall short of adequately delineating this "field" which it is within. So, knowing this, I will continue to stumble along writing here, with the aim to extract and share some useful applications from our "spiritual sensibilities."

~~~~

Why bring the concept of spirituality into a conversation about communication? Because it can be incredibly helpful in elevating the quality of the communication itself. Spiritual is that which is beyond self. Conscious communication requires both an awareness of *and* an elevation beyond self.

Through various forms of contemplation, meditation, and psychedelic exploration, people have reported experiences of "being as Consciousness," and relegating the ego to a back seat in the vehicle of their experience, losing the sense of being the subject in the center of everything—a spiritual experience.

For the sake of simplifying what I'm talking about, I will call the part of us that has these experiences the "spirit." Let's place spirit at the other end of AD (apparent duality) from ego. It's helpful to imagine (and/or believe) that, as ego is me-centric, spirit is we-centric. As ego is fueled by fear, spirit is fueled by love. As ego resists change, spirit embraces change. As ego is defensive, spirit has nothing to defend. As ego understands itself in separation from everything else, for the spirit, we are all one.

As the spirit is nonphysical, the ego exists in the physical thoughts—the electrochemical firings through the neurons and across the synapses in our brain. Ego is in our thoughts. Perhaps spirit emerges in the prior condition of consciousness and is more easily noticed in the brief absences of thought. (By the way, if you find the topic of consciousness particularly interesting, you might enjoy reading Annaka Harris's book *Conscious: A Brief Guide to the Fundamental Mystery of the Mind*. I highly recommend it. Also, her husband, Sam Harris, explores this conversation with great depth and clarity in his books and his mindfulness app, *Waking Up*.)

Neither of these human aspects is better or worse than the other. Both ego and spirit are obviously supposed to be a part of how we roll, simply because they both exist (AD). However, through expanding our awareness of both, and by developing the abilities and functionalities of our minds, we can greatly improve our ability to communicate more consciously.

If someone is trying to communicate with you, and you can move beyond your ego to a place of being focused on the greater good (serving the purpose of the comms), this can be a spiritual experience. Losing "oneself" is a temporary experience of attention being shifted from "how this is about me" to "this is about us all." Spiritual.

The applications of this ability are wide and varied. In our closest personal relationships, the ability to be able to move beyond ego and listen to your partner with complete presence and connection is one of the deepest forms of intimacy. In a work context, the ability to put your defensive ego agenda to the side and listen mindfully and completely to a colleague is not only functional, but can in a sense be termed "spiritual" (beyond self).

As a leader or manager, your ability to connect authentically with someone in your team while coaching or listening to them is an invaluable way for them to feel significant, valued, heard, and engaged. Likewise, as a parent with your children, just five minutes of completely conscious, connected communication with your child is worth hours of distracted, not-really-present time. A spiritual experience.

Have you ever been in the presence of a keynote speaker at an event and felt yourself swept up in the combined emotion of the crowd? Or at a concert, seeing a favorite band lose themselves in the music, bringing the audience with them, and together the collective is as one in communal ecstasy? Upon reflection afterwards, perhaps in telling the story to someone else, you may recall that it felt like you were completely "lost in the moment." What was lost in the moment was just your ego, your sense of being a separate entity. In fact, you were completely in the moment, not in the thoughts of past or future. Not even really in "thoughts" at all. Simply in the moment. These are also examples of communication that became a spiritual experience. Your ego was temporarily nowhere to be found.

Of course, as I have previously alluded to, both aspects of being human are important and are needed at times. As with other parts of life, with ego and spirit, we show up in any given moment somewhere on the spectrum from one extreme to the other, and anywhere in between.

You can be very present for another person in comms and still be aware of yourself. You can listen with curiosity and seek to understand, and still be aware of your point of view. You can even be necessarily defensive, coming from a strong place of ego, creating boundaries to protect yourself, *and* be conscious and aware at the same time. It doesn't need to be one or the other, and perhaps there is more functionality somewhere in the middle than out at the extremes.

How to Bring Spirituality to Comms

If spirituality is the acknowledgment of there being more to life than meets the eye, the acceptance that we are a part of a much bigger collective, and that everything is connected, then the practice of spirituality in communication can start with simply the awareness of this.

Prior to engaging in communication, remember a spiritual perspective. Remind yourself you are an infinitesimally small part of the greater system. Remember that there are things you can't explain and points of view different to yours that are just as valid. Seek to understand, truly understand, the other person or people involved. Practice compassion.

One way to move toward a sense of where someone is coming from is to initially and briefly match their physiology (just for a short period of time). This is a technique to build deep rapport as well. Match their pace, how quickly or slowly they are talking or moving. Match their breathing (this is quite an exquisite practice to employ when in an embrace with your lover). Match their position and posture; if they are sitting, sit; if they lean in, you do too. Of course, you will do this all subtly, so as not to distract! And by the way, humans do this naturally and subconsciously to a degree already.

The practice of matching and mirroring the other person is not always appropriate. Sometimes, if the person you are communicating with is agitated, it may serve better for you to be the opposite: calm, grounded, and centered. Trust your innate sensibility when deciding what's best going to serve the moment, but remember to have the courage to try techniques consciously with the intention of facilitating better communication.

The right amount of quality eye contact is also a way to connect more deeply with someone in communication. Avoiding eye contact can send signals of perhaps having something to hide, or disinterest, or being distracted. Too much eye contact can be unnerving; intense eye contact can seem invasive. A practice to achieve functional eye contact is to "come from a good place." If your intentions are to make the person feel heard and that you care, if you genuinely seek to understand and respect them, your eye contact will be like magic. The communication will be conscious. The connection may well become spiritual.[4]*

---

4 * Remember to be mindful of times when your ego tries to derail any of the above processes. If you're worried about how you will look, or if you're justifying to yourself not trying these practices, that's your ego making it all about you. Your spirit doesn't mind about "looking good;" your spirit is in the experience of connection.

Chapter Seven

NONVERBAL COMMUNICATION

I t was a warm day in Mysore, south Indian winter and dry season. The blue skies were lightly speckled with small, wispy white clouds, letting through enough sun warmth with intermittent cloud shade relief. The sounds of the marketplace, the smells of Indian spices on display, the meandering cows and cheeky monkeys kicking back in the trees, all were comforting me as I wandered through town in search of a chai. It was relaxed here. So different from the pace of the big cities.

I had been traveling solo for a few months and had become content in my own company. I could go where I wanted, whenever I wanted, without needing to check in with, or take into account, anyone else. Aahhhhhh, barefoot backpacking freedom.

I had no agenda. No time frame. Nowhere to be. Plenty of time to smoke hashish, contemplate the mysteries of life, and play my guitar. I was in the midst of my first identity crisis/opportunity year and loving it. The pangs of my broken heart were more like occasional whispers now; *I wonder who she's with. I wonder where she is.*

The soles of my feet were toughened up enough from my barefoot wanderings, and I was happy having as few possessions as possible. My wardrobe consisted of a couple of *lungis* (a large piece of material men wrap around themselves like a full-length skirt) and a couple of tees. I had some flip-flops for times when shoes were required, but they spent most of their time strapped to my small pack.

My dreadlocks and beard were long enough now that locals could put me in either of two pigeonholes: strange-looking sadhu wandering around India seeking spiritual enlightenment, or Western hippie kinda doing the same thing. Neither of these categories was at all threatening, enticing, or necessarily attractive, so I pretty much got left alone. Beggars didn't even ask me for anything anymore.

On this day, I found myself wandering out of the center of town, toward the hill on the outskirts and the old temple at the top. I don't even remember spending much time at the temple itself. I certainly wouldn't have lined up with the Indian tourists to pay an entrance fee and go inside. I think I was probably "templed out" by then.

What I do remember is the few hours I spent sitting on a rock off the beaten track, on the far side of the hill. I was meditating, eyes open, gazing up at the sky, when a young boy came and sat next to me in silence. I turned to him, and we made eye contact. The hint of a smile moved on both our faces, and I returned to my skygazing. He was dressed as simply as me, denoting his lower-caste status, but his energy was that of a wise old sage.

He sat with me for about an hour. Not a word was spoken, but galaxies were understood. What I felt communicated was two-way acceptance, admiration, reverence and love. Time seemed to almost stop. It was completely comfortable. Then, when our time together was done, he rose, we looked into each other's eyes for only the second time, we hinted at a smile, and then he left. Special, nonverbal connection.

That night I decided to pack my stuff and get on the next train. As was my preference at the time, I didn't purchase a ticket for a seat, but found myself a spot on the floor with the poorest passengers, just outside the toilets by the open carriage door. The warm breeze of the rural Indian night was enough to remove the stench from the loo, as I sat shoulder to shoulder with my traveling companions. To my left was the open door and the monotonous clickety-clack of the passing tracks and world outside. To my immediate right was a mother with her three little ones. Through the hours of that night, we communicated and formed a bond with not a word spoken.

The communication included nonverbal dialogue like this.

"Do you mind my children climbing on you?"

"No, that's fine."

"Eat some of our nuts and seeds."

"Okay, thank you."

"You are a nice man."

"Thank you. Your children are cute."

"They are tired now. We've been traveling a long time."

"This one can sleep in my arms."

"That is no problem?"

"No, sister, no problem, it's fine."

This communication was all through gestures and eye contact. In the early morning hour, just prior to dawn, when the dark first moved toward light, the train slowed at a small village station. This was one of the places where the train doesn't actually come to a halt, but just slows to a brisk walking pace while passengers climb on and jump off.

My traveling companion gathered up her baggage and children and, as she was climbing over me to the open door, she reached her hand down with a smile. In my half-sleep delirium, I thought she was saying, "*Namaste*, goodbye," and wanting to shake my hand, so I reached out and took her hand. It was then that she pushed a ten-rupee note into my hand. She was giving me money! She was doing what they did in their culture: financially supporting a man on his spiritual quest to free himself of his worldly possessions and travel the land seeking enlightenment.

"*Nahin, didi!!*" (No, sister!) I exclaimed, too late. She had vanished with her kids into the approaching dawn as the train gathered speed again, taking me onwards to gather my thoughts. She had given me what was, to her, enough to feed the kids a meal. And I had thousands of dollars in a foreign bank account! For a moment I felt like a fraud, an imposter. I had way more money than she would ever know in her life. But then, as I relaxed back into the clickety-clack rhythm and a traveler's contemplation, I realized how perfect it all was. The night of authentic connection and silent communication with another human, and her parting gesture of support: *I see you*, I heard her say; *Namaste*.

There are many times in life when nonverbal communication is more appropriate, and even necessary. Sometimes your loved one just wants to put their head on your chest and have you hold them in your arms. The wordless but conscious communication can be, *I've got you. You're safe. Everything is okay.*

Perhaps a work colleague is about to stand up and present to the team. You can sense they are nervous and worried about how their ideas will be received. They look over to you for reassurance, and in the silence of your smile and warm eyes, you let them know they are going to be fine.

In the depth of grief and loss, when there are no words to console, simply sitting in silence with that person can communicate everything they need in that moment. There have been many playful conversations had on dance floors, many moments of intimate communication lying silently next to each other in bed. What's most important in these dialogues is where you are coming from. Again, it comes back to your intention. For what purpose are you engaged in this communication? And how can you be more consciously so?

I've been running a Conscious Leadership program in the Himalaya since 2014 where we take Western leaders deep into the mountains and way off the grid. When I first had the notion to take people there, back in 1998, and I shared the idea with my mountain brother, Pappu, he said to me, "It is a wonderful idea. Why don't we pick up rubbish while we are trekking in the mountains?"

Sixteen years later, the seed became a tree and bore fruit. The interesting thing is that we've found the most effective way to have our clients pick up rubbish is not to tell them to do so, but simply to do it ourselves. Early in our week of walking, people are picking up rubbish and keeping it in their pockets or packs until the end of the day, when we transfer it into the empty garbage bags we've brought. Then our packhorses carry it the rest of the way! All without asking anyone to do anything! Nonverbal communication. Leading by example.

One client took this initiative as far as sending money from Australia to sponsor the village locals to install bins in the town and set up a rubbish collection and education program.

Quite often, the profound can be accessed more easily in the spaces we create between talking. On day five of the program, when we are gathered around the morning fire, drinking chai and eating porridge, I let the group know that this day is a day of silence. We spend the day, until dinner time, not uttering a word, and walking *very* slowly. Initially, a lot of our clients struggle internally with this, but one by one, all of them "pop" into the meditative flow state. We are deep and high in remote mountains. The views are breathtaking. The air is clean. The eagles soaring above us are majestic. The silence is stunning. Pappu and I communicate when and where to stop for lunch and breaks with no words. At the end of the day, when we gather wood and light the fire, then gently introduce words back into the group, everybody, in their own way, comes to let me know that was one of the most profound days of their life.

There are certainly times for silence, and the nonverbal conscious communication in these times can be a special, even spiritual, experience.

Chapter Eight

THE COMMS YOU DON'T WANT TO HAVE

It was a Thursday night, April 8, 2010. It must have been about ten o'clock. My six- and four-year-old sons were in bed, fast asleep, and I had just retired to mine as well. My wife was away interstate on a well-needed break. The phone rang. I ignored it. It rang again and I looked. It was Mum. Unusual for her to call at this hour.

"Hello, Mum?"

...pause...

"Tim is dead."

"What?"

"Tim died on his motorbike this evening."

Still, to this day, this has been the worst night of my life. I am the eldest of four kids. Tim was the youngest. We always were, and still are, a very close family. The love runs deep and unconditionally. My siblings are among my closest friends.

A year before, we had been given the news that my dad had a brain tumor. Despite the surgeries and treatments, a year is all he ended up having. Dad was only sixty-seven when he died in the December just before, and the rest of us rallied from around the world (we've all spent many years working and living in different countries) to be with him through palliative care at home. His death was actually quite beautiful, with us all around his bed for his last breath and release from suffering.

Tim and his wife had been living in Canada, and they'd decided to move back to Australia to be with Mum. "I want to come and look after you, Mum," he'd said. Dad's death, as sad as it was, made sense. He was the generation above. They're supposed to go first, right? We knew it was coming. No shock or surprise there. Tim's death four months later was the opposite. All wrong. Not supposed to be. Completely shocking and gut-wrenchingly painful. Leaving a recently widowed mum to deal with losing her youngest child.

I'm not sure which end of the communication is harder—having to say those words, or to hear them. I can't remember much detail from the moment I heard the news, but I had to go from receiver to giver of this information pretty much straight away, and call my wife to let her know. I can't really remember making that call. Hardly "conscious communication."

The thought of telling our sons was unfathomable initially. They adored their Uncle Tim. Thankfully, my parents-in-law were able to step in and be with the kids while I jumped on the next available flight to my home state. Their grandparents told them he'd had an accident and was in hospital, and I had gone to be with him.

The next few weeks were an onslaught of what seemed like interminable tidal waves—mountains of pain shuddering through every part of our beings, as we communicated our collective disbelief and loss, anger and refusal, and rage at the unfairness of his death.

I had grown up in an open-door household. Everyone was welcome, and people were always coming and going, visiting and staying. It was no different in grieving. Tim was larger than life. He was that star shining its brightest just before expiring. His death rocked many lives, from many walks of life and many corners of the earth. Every time the next person fell through the front door, collapsing in their part of our collective mess, we would fall with them and wail all over again.

The communication was in many forms: from physical and verbal through to silence and stillness, from acts of service to nurturing care. We were cooked for and fed. The household chores were taken care of. We prepared for the second family funeral in a few months. And it was all on a foundation of Love.

~~~~~~

Sometimes there is communication that needs to be had that you just don't want to have. I try to live by this adage: "Speak the truth with love and all will be well." Mind you, it's also good to remember that not everything should necessarily be said. There are some "truths" that may not serve the greater good in a given moment.

Letting someone know a loved one has died is an extreme example of difficult comms. There are many times in our lives when something needs to be said, yet we either avoid it or at least procrastinate over it. Why? Well, there could be many reasons. We don't want to upset the person. We don't want to create conflict. We don't want more drama in our life. We are worried the other person will just take it the wrong way. We don't know how to say it. We are not sure if we should communicate this thing. We want to be liked. We don't want to create enemies. And so on.

The first step to take is via the process I have introduced already (and will go into more deeply) in this book. Why? For what purpose would I communicate this? If the tough conversation you are considering having is with intention for the greater good, then it's a conversation you should have. But who decides if it's for the greater good? You do. You need to consider all those concerned, weigh up the outcomes to the best of your ability, and decide whether the net impact outcome is positive or not. If your intentions are for the greater good, then you're good.

You may, however, like a lot of humans, be getting in the way of what is actually for the greater good. You might decide not to have the conversation, having convinced yourself it's for the best, when really, it's just your ego very cleverly justifying not having it, to disguise avoidance. Or alternatively, maybe you just had the conversation for ultimately selfish reasons but convinced yourself it was good for the other person to hear you "get it off [your] chest." You may have been burdening someone with information that didn't benefit them, just to alleviate your sense of guilt.

There is no precise formula that will tell you what to communicate and what not to. You need to look within for the answer and trust yourself. You can get better at this through creating a practice of mindfulness meditation in your life (see Chapter Twelve). I believe we know what the "right thing to do" in situations is. Deep down inside, we have our own moral compass, and for the majority of us, its north is reasonably true. When we can quiet the noise of our busy brains, our identification with "stuff," and our ego, we know what we should do.

You know what you should do.

Having decided to communicate something tough doesn't make it less tough; it just means you can move toward having the conversation. The important thing to remember from this chapter is that when you approach that communication from a place of love—i.e., care, consideration, openness, gentleness, and clarity—know that the end net result will be good. However, this doesn't mean it will necessarily be received well immediately. The person hearing the tough news will react and respond however they do. That part is already in the accept basket. But what you can control is deciding to have the conversation, and what you can influence is the communication itself, by having it consciously, carefully, and with integrity.

In situations where I have to deliver news that's hard to hear, or perhaps confrontational, I find it best to remember "less is more." By this, I mean less words. If you start building up to the point, and take too long skirting around the edges or trying to sugar-coat it, it can easily be construed as condescending. People are smart and sensitive. Honor their innate intelligence and let them know why you're having the conversation. Depending on the context, it can help to simply state where you're coming from or why you're communicating this before you deliver the tough bit. But keep it short, and remember to come from the heart; be completely present, and genuinely care.

A Tough Comms Strategy

I call this strategy "getting the green light." I've been teaching this to leaders and teams for years, and I love it. It is simple and effective. Basically, it is setting up permission with someone to have tough conversations in the future. It's about creating a relationship where both parties understand the benefit of being able to have honest and upfront dialogue if it is to serve the greater good. This can also apply beautifully to the relationship with your partner. Even with family members and friends.

I'll give you an example in the context of leadership. John is the leader of a team, and he understands that part of his role is to help develop and coach the people in his team to be the best they can be, and to continually improve and feel engaged with what they do. John has a team member who reacts defensively every time he tries to offer "constructive criticism." Each time he tries to give feedback, he sees the walls going up, the arms folding across the chest, the eyes rolling, and the not-so-subtle huffs of indignation. What to do?

Let's say the team member's name is Rosie. In a one-on-one conversation, and in a moment when John is *not* giving performance improvement feedback, he could set up the green light something like this:

"Rosie, I just wanted to share with you what I hope for in my role here at [ABC Physio]. A part of my responsibility, and what I care about, is helping you shine. Creating an environment where you feel safe and valued."

"Uh-huh."

"When you're happy—evolving, flourishing, and loving what you do—that's the sweet spot, yeah? When we have the whole team like that, happy days, right?"

"Yeah, absolutely."

"Is it okay with you if I do what I can to help make that happen for you?"

"Yeah, of course, John."

"Because I have to say, I feel like I've let you down in the past."

"Oh, really?"

"Yep. There have been times when I could've offered some guidance to help you in your role, but I didn't because I was worried you'd take it the wrong way."

"Oh."

"I was worried you might take it as a negative, when all I want is to help you shine."

"Oh."

"If it's okay with you, I'd like to promise you that, from now on, I will have the courage to come forward and offer you ideas on how you can continue to grow in your role and love your job. Is that okay?"

"Yeah, of course, John. I always want to get better at what I do."

John now has the green light from Rosie to give feedback. I don't recommend then launching immediately into constructive criticism (and probably avoid using that terminology), but the next time John needs to communicate feedback, it will be easier than before.

Occasionally, even when you've done your best to frame the green light in a way that shows what's in it for them, you will get people who refuse to be open to feedback. If this is the case in a professional setting, then perhaps they are on the wrong bus, and you need to be thinking about how to help them off at the next stop!

My partner and I have a version of this green light strategy in our relationship. When we first got together, we had wonderful conversations about what didn't work for us in our past relationships. The last thing either of us wanted was to find ourselves looping in old, dysfunctional broken records!

Something we had both experienced was a feeling of being on eggshells around our previous partners—worried that we might say something that would upset them and cause an argument. So, we had found ourselves in relationships where we would sometimes hold back from speaking our truth so as not to break more eggs.

To avoid this happening again for us, we agreed that one of the pillars of our relationship would be IT—immediate truth. We promised we would share our truth with each other, even if it might be uncomfortable. And we promised to hear each other with an open heart and to not break eggs, but just listen and seek to understand. It works wonderfully. And it is *such* a relief to be just walking on floorboards at home now, with no eggshells between our toes!

Chapter Nine

NITTY GRITTY

The Communication
of Consent

The producer timed it so that, before each performance, he would come in to "wish me good luck for the show" when I was naked. He would hang out in my dressing room for too long and say sleazy, inappropriate things to me. I was eighteen. He was fifty. I was naive, and like a deer in the headlights with my first professional acting job. He was an "experienced" individual with a penchant for perversion, who'd been around the block more than a few times.

Despite feeling awkward, uncomfortable, and disgusted, and wishing he would leave me alone, I didn't say, "I want you to stop." We were touring regional theatres for months. I endured it and stayed silent. I really wanted the work, and was obviously hoping for more acting gigs after that one. He had some sort of power, and he knew it.

Did my silence mean I gave him consent?

By now, I'm hoping there is a message starting to appear in the pages of this book. Conscious communication is about the greater good of all concerned, not just about an individual's agenda with disregard for anyone else. It simply must be at least a two-way— or when more people are involved, a multi-directional—flow of energy. Hearing and seeking to understand the other(s) involved, even if they are silent, is as important as speaking.

You would think that, in the context of violation of a person, this should be pretty clear-cut and straightforward, but apparently, it's not. The mixed-up, dysfunctional messages our boys and young men receive, through relentless broadcasting from outdated culture, certainly muddy the waters and can give them very wrong ideas.

Before I start talking about the questions I've asked myself and the conversations I've had about sex and consent, I want to bring up this point: having someone's consent should be considered across the board in all contexts. In all forms of communication, whether it be verbal, physical, emotional, energetic, sexual, or otherwise.

There are times, however, when I communicate without necessarily having consent, usually as a parent. When one of my kids crosses a clear boundary, they may not want me to come into their room and communicate the consequences that are being applied for a particular action. Is this communication without consent? I guess so. What I have noticed, however, is that if I can manage to have some sort of consent, instead of defiance, in those conversations, the end result is always better.

"Hey, mate, I need to come in and have a chat with you about one of the choices you made today. Is that okay with you?"

"Yeah, okay, Dad."

Consent. Not always that easy to get, and sometimes, as a parent, we just have to communicate without the "Okay, Dad," regardless. But I always get a better result if I have some sort of green light to the conversation.

I can't think of any situations when communicating without consent is better than with. You might be at the end of your tether with your partner; perhaps there has been something gnawing away at you for too long. You've tried to communicate it, but they keep shutting it down. They just don't want to hear it. Then finally you explode, the levee breaks, and you can't stop the gushing torrents of expression as you raise your voice in exasperation. Perhaps they start shouting back, or just shut down and zip up the impenetrable walls around them. Either way, your good intention to communicate how you feel for the "greater good" of the relationship has been lost in what has become unconscious communication. An unfortunate outburst and subsequent outcome.

Finding a way to your partner's consent for the communication is giving the relationship a *much* better chance of remaining conscious and moving toward mutual understanding and healing. In a moment when things are calm, and no one's in a hurry to be somewhere else, it could be something like this:

"[My love], our relationship is my home base. I want to honor you and our relationship. I want to always get better at communicating with you, because you deserve to be in a trusting and transparent partnership. It's sometimes hard for me to express how I feel, but I'd like to try now. Would that be okay with you?"

If your version of this framing question ends up with a yes, you have comms consent, and a much better chance of success.

So now we come to the most important—and, sadly, still the most relevant—conversation when we talk about consent: in the context of having sex. The idea, to me, of having sex with someone who doesn't want it is so completely foreign and abhorrent that to say it turns me *off* is an understatement. My past "hang-ups" around this have led to a whole other, more intricate conversation I want to share with you in this chapter. But first I must state the obvious, because you might find it hard to believe, but there are still a lot of men out there who missed this memo—having (forcing) sex with (on) anyone without their consent is *completely wrong*, horrible, dysfunctional, criminal, messed-up, and something we, as a society, should be doing everything we can to stop.

Not giving consent doesn't need to be verbal. Silence doesn't necessarily mean consent! Coercion doesn't mean consent. Saying yes initially, and then changing their mind, doesn't mean consent. Falling asleep or passing out *does not* mean consent. Consent is only when the other person wants it, wholeheartedly let's-go-there-give-it-to-me wants it. Simple as that.

That now said, I want to speak about more subtle and trickier navigations through the intimate communication of consent within a functional relationship, i.e., where there is no abuse. As someone who is aroused by my partner's enjoyment, by her desire, by her pleasure, by her consent, not only do we *not* make love if she doesn't want to, I've had to learn how to not be too cautious in any initiation. I used to worry about upsetting her or coming across as just another sex-crazed guy, so I would almost tiptoe into sex. And then, in some of our conversations, she would tell me that sometimes she just wants me to "take her" (but only when there's consent!).

I have had to learn (and now continue to practice) how to access my functional masculine assertiveness in the initiation. How to fine-tune my conscious awareness to her cycle and sensitivities. How to read her quite often nonverbal communication of "yes" or "no." I find it easier to spend time slowly warming her up, honoring her Feminine and building the sexual fire. I find it harder to just grab her and jolt her out of wherever she is at, to "have my way with her."

I have to practice not taking it personally when I've picked the wrong moment. The times when I misread the play and thought, "I'm just going to grab her and kiss her and take her," but she lets me know, "Now's not the time, my love." Of course, I never persist in these moments. Like I said, it turns me right off if my partner is not turned on, but the internal communication with self (remember that from earlier chapters?) now has the opportunity to be curated. *Hey, Jem, it's okay. You had the courage to put yourself out there. You've communicated that you want her, that you find her attractive. Now find another way to show her you love her.*

I know of relationships where one person submits to sex more than they would like, just to keep their partner happy. They give consent, but then resent. Their more sexually driven partner, who insists on a certain frequency of sexual encounters, not only pressures for consent, but expects the other to "want it" as much as them.

Is this consent? Starts to get grey, huh? Especially if the submissive partner says, "I don't really mind. It keeps him happy, and the sex ends up being good even when I don't initially feel like it."

The balance and communication of consent in a non-abusive, reasonably functional relationship can still be a sensitive subject. When in doubt, talk about it. Seek to understand. Share your vulnerabilities. Set up some signals between the two of you to make it easier to know when, without having to ask, "Do you want to have sex?" Give and get permission to be human and get it wrong sometimes, and remember that in those moments, the love and conscious communication of such is the higher ground.

Chapter Ten

DEEPER MEN-WITH-MEN COMMUNICATION

The arrivals hall of the Islamabad International Airport was packed with a sea of bearded men in plain-colored shalwar kameez. I was one of them. Aussie man blended in. I had been in Pakistan for about a week, awaiting the arrival of my brother, whom I hadn't seen for over two years. It was hot and humid. The air was heavy. A cacophony of subcontinent sounds and smells made its way inside the hall.

For a few days, I had been preparing for his arrival. I was camped in a city park designated for travelers and refugees. I found a stack of extra cardboard boxes to use as a mattress, I had bought a mosquito net and some twine to string it to trees, and I had splashed out and bought some Afghani opium for us as a treat. I was stocked up on tea, veggies, and rice, and enough spices. I wanted to make our reunion special.

When my brother emerged through the sliding doors from immigration and out into the arrivals hall, he scanned the sea of olive-skinned, bearded men and missed me on the first pass. It was only on his second and more intent search, when he caught a glint of the silver piercings through my lower lip (remnants of my London punk days), buried in my beard, that he recognized me.

Smiles cracked our faces open wide as we beelined to each other and hugged tightly. There were no words—not yet. We grabbed his pack in smiling silence and walked arm in arm to a taxi. The whole taxi ride was just one big smiling, silent, happy, brotherly reconnection. It wasn't until I walked him through the campsite to our mosquito-net abode, and the opium began to do its thing, that we started talking. And then we didn't stop.

It wasn't just two years to catch up on, it was two of the biggest years for each of us. I was twenty-seven and he was twenty-three. He had become a father since we'd last seen each other, and I had been reborn through heartbreak, ego death, and reidentification. We had both been traveling through very foreign lands, but the conversation lasted through the night and the whole of the next day, not because we were just swapping the "what happened" notes, but because we were diving into the "how was that for you?" underneath each experience. "How did that make you feel?" "What did that mean for you?" "Was that a struggle?" "How are you healing?" We shared our philosophical ideas and our resilience strategies. We pondered the biggest questions and gave thanks for the smallest graces. We talked and listened and listened and talked. I will remember that reunion forever.

As I look back now, it's clear that my relationship with both of my brothers, and the quality of our conversations and connections, formed the foundation of my ability to communicate deeply and authentically with other men. I most probably took it for granted when I was younger and became friends with males like me. So, in my younger version of reality, that's just how men were—able to talk deeply and share their emotions. It wasn't until I started to explore more widely and meet a broader cross-section of males that I began to realize perhaps it's not the norm.

Through my work, I have met many men who never talk with their mates in a space of vulnerability. It's all bravado and brave face, until they get enough beers in them and a switch flicks, then it's all a slobbery, messy, "I laarrvv youuuuu!!!!" "Nahhhh, I reeeaaaallly faarkin luv youuuu, maaate!!" with the next morning leaving not even a vague, dusty trace of having "opened up."

When I talk with men who are not used to speaking deeply with their mates, and let them know about things like men's circle, initially they can be somewhat bemused: "You do what?"

"We sit around a fire once a month. No booze. No smoking. We pick a meaningful theme to talk about and then take turns to go around the circle and share what it is for us. It's not a counselling session. It's not a complaining session. It's just a safe and confidential space to share your deepest experience of something and feel heard and not judged."

The concept and practice are completely foreign to a lot of men, but interestingly enough, often pique interest and curiosity.

"If I came along, would I have to speak if I didn't want to?"

I think men quietly crave authentic connection and validation with and from each other. The camaraderie of a sporting team or an interest club is palpable. Sadly, because of our outdated and irrelevant culture, the conversations stay at a surface level and are not encouraged to go any deeper. "Don't worry, mate. You deserve better. You'll be right. Just pick yourself up and get on with it. Carn mate. Let's just go have a kick of the footy, then a couple a beers at the local. Don't fuckin' worry about it!" (All said with the best intention of wanting to help a mate feel better!)

Imagine if it was more normal for the friend to say, "Geez, that must really hurt, mate. You loved her so much and now she's left you. How are you feeling?" "I'm here, mate, better to let it out than bottle it all up. You can talk about anything with me, I've got ya. I understand if you don't feel like going out tonight. Do you want some company at your place?"

It comes back to the chapter on being an island. Men don't just become islands from their partners, they become islands from their mates too. It's this false notion that I must be the only one who goes through this. Every other bloke seems on top of their game. Every other bloke has got it together. Then the shame sets in. I'm a freak. There's something wrong with me. No one else would understand. Island.

I was genuinely surprised, when I finally had the courage to speak up about my anxieties with sex, by the number of men who would say to me, "Brother, you too? I've had my own version of that going on and I haven't told anyone!" In a tantric workshop many years ago, I shared my story and subsequent healing process. Several men approached me afterwards to say thank you and ask for advice. One of them I coached for three months and helped him on his road to liberate himself from that suffering. Who knows, maybe if I hadn't spoken up, he might still be stuck.

How to Create Change

It starts with you. If you think there are times when you hold back from venturing a bit deeper into a conversation with a mate, have the courage to go there. Chances are he will respond positively, and the conversation will multiply in value for both of you.

If you are a man who speaks openly, authentically, and vulnerably already, who are the men around you that you could encourage and help come to this in themselves?

I believe that those of us who are in some way connected to any basic sense of what's okay and what's not, in terms of the way we treat ourselves and other people, on some level know when we are caught up in a peer-group or indoctrinated behavior that's dysfunctional. Deep down, we know when we are behaving in a way that's not okay, but the denial and defense, the justification and confirmation bias processes, are so successful at keeping us from our truth.

Conscious conversations can set us free. Start them. Talk about human stuff. Talk about your struggles. Talk about your joys. Ask your friends about what it's really like for them and seek to understand. Men are responsible for almost all of the violence globally—domestic, societal, and political. It's time we took responsibility for our collective and encourage our fellow men to evolve. The power of conscious conversations is an essential part of paving this way forward.

Part III

COMMS TOOLS

Chapter Eleven

LETTING GO

I barely had a chance to catch a flash of the big, Indian Ambassador automobile as it came hurtling out of a laneway between two buildings to knock me off my Enfield motorbike. I wasn't wearing a helmet at the time, and my head hit the asphalt hard. All went black.

The year was 1998, and I was riding my motorbike north from Delhi to Rishikesh in time for the largest gathering of humans anywhere on the planet, the Kumbh Mela. The immediate problem for me to solve was the fact that I was now badly injured, in a small village with no hospital. My motorbike was almost as damaged as me, and only one local spoke any English: the doctor leaning in to inject me with something as I regained consciousness, dazed and confused. He wasn't the only one in his treatment room; it was jam-packed with curious local men, squashed together around my bed and peering over each other to stare at this strange and injured man from a foreign land.

The first words to come from me were, "*Whoa!!!* Wait! What is that?" as I pointed to the syringe in his hand. "This is a tetanus shot, *ji*. You have been badly hurt." I quickly managed enough clarity, perhaps from shock and adrenaline, to remove my travel wallet from inside my shirt and produce my vaccination card, showing a recent tetanus shot. The doctor acknowledged this with a short, half head-wobble, then began preparing another syringe, making sure to show me it was a clean instrument and advising me this one was painkiller. "Yes please, I have a feeling I'm gonna need that."

After establishing, in broken Hindi, with the small sea of men surrounding me, that the culprit had fled the scene directly after running me over, I insisted they leave the room and give me some space to gather myself. There was no mirror, but a slow and careful touch check over my body told me my head and face were completely bandaged, as too were my hands, feet, and left knee. Blood was seeping through in all these places. Shit. This ain't good.

Then I remembered my bike, with all my belongings. A lot of my travel funds were invested in that Enfield, and everything I owned was strapped to it. I eased myself off the bed and, to the protestations of the nurse, made my way outside the GP clinic. Most of the townsfolk were there, all gathered round to get a look at me, and proudly present my broken bike and all my belongings they had gathered from the accident scene and brought to the patch of dirt outside the clinic. My heartfelt namaste displayed my thanks to all.

The town's only Enfield mechanic and his son were patiently waiting in the wings, knowing I'd need them next. The moment my thoughts went to fixing the bike, they both rose from their squatted position in the dirt and made their way through the crowd to me. We communicated with agreeing head wobbles and namastes, then the dad pushed my bike and the boy put me on the back of his to take me to their shop.

As they got to work dismantling and repairing on tarpaulins in the dirt on the side of the road, I limped off in search of a pharmacy. This little mission confirmed that this was a small village, and not somewhere I wanted to get stuck when the pain kicked in and I was immobilized. As soon as the bike was fixed and paid for, I mounted my steed and made for the Himalayan foothills.

I must've looked quite alarming, bandaged up and covered in blood as I rode the four hours to my destination; I turned every head in each town I passed. Every policeman tried in vain to wave me down. I wasn't stopping for anyone.

The last part of my journey, after riding through Rishikesh and up to Laxman Jhula, was to walk my bike across the narrow, swinging rope bridge of that name. The bridge was busy with beggars and pilgrims, and it took almost the last of my reserves to get through the throng to the other side.

"Cross the bridge and turn left" had been the instructions given to me by a French-Canadian travel friend, who for this book I will call Isabelle. "Just down the way you will see Bombay Guest House. That is where I'll be." And that is where she was, thank the gods! As I entered through the front gate archway and into the open courtyard, the owner came rushing toward me, shouting, "No, we are full! We don't have room for you here!" (I must've looked like trouble.) As he began to usher me backward, Isabelle appeared from her room. "Jem! My God! *Putain de merde*! What the fuck happened to you?"

"I had an accident."

"Yeah, no shit." Then Isabelle turned to the hotel owner and ordered, "He is staying with me, get me some more bedding, some clean water, and a towel. Go! Now! *Chalo!*"

What followed from that evening on, as I lived and healed in the Bombay Guest House over the next month, was nothing short of miraculous. The communication, connection, contribution, and community that formed around me became the foundation of an accelerated healing experience. Pivotal to this was my ability to let go and surrender to the experience.

At the center of this healing tribe was an English senior nurse, backpacking with her four-year-old daughter. I'll call her Julie in this story, but will always remember her and her daughter's real names. We had met six months prior, down the other end of India, on a train journey. I had helped her get her bags and daughter up onto the train at a rural station with no platform. We then enjoyed conversation and company for a few hours before parting ways and not seeing each other again, until now.

After Isabelle had supported me to her room, which conveniently had two single beds in it, she suggested I lie down, but as soon as I was on the bed, I knew I might very well be bedridden for some time, and so replied, "I think I need to get some food into me to fuel this healing."

"Across the way is a restaurant, you will be okay to get there?"

"I think I'll be fine. Thank you so much, Isabelle. I am super grateful I found you and you've taken me in."

"But of course." She smiled empathetically. "I'll be here when you get back." Her French-Canadian accent soothed me.

As I made my way into the restaurant perched above the powerful Ganges River, still in the same bloodied clothes and bandages, I saw Julie and her daughter exiting after their meal. It took Julie a moment to recognize me beneath my Halloween disguise; then, from that moment on, I became the recipient of the most generous time of contribution and care I have ever received.

Not only was Julie a highly qualified Western nurse, she was also a reiki master practitioner and had a heart of gold. She dedicated hours each day over the following weeks to clean and dress my wounds, giving hands-on energy healing as well. Initially I tried to refuse taking so much of her time, urging her to leave me, and assuring her that I would be okay. On the third day, she looked me sternly in the eyes and said, "Stop being so stubborn. Let go. Soften and receive!"

This advice has not only stuck with me all these years, but has been such "translate-able gold," working in many different situations.

Then word began to spread. The travelers and locals alike did what we humans do. They communicated and contributed. I had all sorts of alternative healers from different modalities coming to lend a hand: a German magnet therapist, a Kiwi kinesiologist, two Italian brothers who would come each day to carry me down to the holy Ganga for the purifying water, random travelers who heard I was running out of swabs and brought theirs to donate, spiritual healers and musicians, mindfulness teachers, and more. I said yes to it all. I said yes to receiving the communication of care and healing. I said yes to letting go.

Early in the recovery process, Julie had voiced her concern at the extent of the injuries. Half of the skin from my face had been torn off on the road, and there were deep gouges running down my temple and the bridge of my nose. "Jem, I think we should take you to hospital." I didn't have travel insurance back then, and I had already had some reasonably horrific experiences in Indian public hospitals. I said I would prefer to heal there in the Bombay Guest House, connected to community and away from death and disease.

"As long as you remain free from infection, I'm okay with that. But if I see even a hint of infection, you are off to hospital."

On day ten of the healing, Julie removed the dressing and a look of disbelief I will always remember came over her face. "What?" I asked, slightly worried. "Is there infection?"

"No," Julie said, still in a state of surprise. "In all my years of nursing, I have never seen skin regenerate and heal like this, and this quickly. This is truly quite amazing."

In the first week after the accident, one of the things I had come to terms with was that I would probably be quite facially scarred for life from the injuries. I guess I can't be disappointed that I've only ended up with two slight scars that are easily missed without closer inspection.

This whole accident and healing experience was many things: a story of surrender and acceptance, one of connection and of how it "takes a village." It was my time to learn how to let go and welcome the miracles that can come from others, *and* (here comes the AD) to assimilate that with my own completely personal power-of-the-mind work. I was connected, and I was alone. Not one person there did I know well or have I stayed in touch with, but I was completely with them at the time.

~~~

You may be wondering how this story relates to Conscious Communication. Perhaps you have your own intuitions as to how already. It's simply this: *let go*. When you hold on too tightly to anything (including how you think communication should go), you are closed off to alternative possibilities to which you were previously blind. You are placing limitations on Potential and Possibility.

Soften your grip. Let go of some of your determined direction. Allow the input of others. Consider that which seems counterintuitive. Relax, breathe, and create space for the "miracles" that can occur from true collaboration.

Let's look at some practical examples and applications of this.

Imagine you and your partner are disagreeing. They have a completely different point of view than you. You are determined you are right and you know best this time, as you've been there before! You learnt the hard way and now you know "the truth" of the matter (sound familiar?). So, rather than dig your heels in and demand they listen to you for their own good (I mean, you're only trying to help them anyway, right?), what might happen if you paused, car-parked your "truth" for a moment and really leant into what they were trying to say? Listen to their alternate reality, not to disprove it, but to really try and seek to understand, to put yourself in their shoes and get where they are coming from.

This doesn't mean their point of view will necessarily be the outcome. That's not actually the point. But imagine the quality and tone of the communication once you soften and become present to your partner. It is in this state of Conscious Communication that the best, blended way forward from the disagreement will be allowed to emerge.

By the way, letting go doesn't mean resignation, giving in, giving up, or switching off! You will get a completely different reaction if you do that in the conversation, just saying, "Yes, dear, you're right." Humans' perception is way too finely tuned to be able to pull that wool over anyone's eyes.

Besides, when you do that, there's a good chance you are being passive-aggressive (ever been called that before? Eeeek), and you want them to know that on some level you still disagree. Not only does this leave a residue of resentment between you, it's also energetically unattractive and unsexy!

Let's look at another scenario. You are the more experienced team member in a problem-solving situation at work, not just marginally, but by many years. Perhaps your fellow team member is a junior, still in their novice years. You may very well know the tried and tested solutions, but what if the novice felt allowed to offer crazy ideas, unbound by the knowledge of "what's not possible?" What if one of those crazy ideas actually sparked innovation and a genius solution? The genius would be possible because you created space for it by letting go.

Even if their ideas couldn't work that time, the relationship you're building and the team culture you are cultivating will be way more conducive to future collaborations and healthier working dynamics.

So how do you do this? By remembering to "let go." Let go of being the expert. Let go of your grip on "how things should be." Let go of needing to win and be the one who worked it out. Let go of "things having to go exactly to plan." Think about it: when you look back, has anything ever gone exactly to plan, down to the last minute detail? Even the best-laid plans very rarely "go to plan!" Seems crazy to hold on tightly to something that isn't likely to happen, huh?

Chapter Twelve

MINDFULNESS IN COMMUNICATION

Have you ever left a heated or emotional conversation feeling like you lost some control of yourself in the moment? Have you ever reflected and realized you were completely reactionary and perhaps unnecessarily defensive? Have you ever left a conversation with things left unsaid? Words that gnaw at you and tumble together with your question, "Why didn't I say what I really wanted to?"

How many of these times do you feel you got the best result as far as the communication was concerned? If the communication purpose was to resolve an issue, convey information, be understood, or reach understanding, the chances are...not many.

If, however, the purpose was for the other person to see you emotional, then you were probably successful, and this context of communication is sometimes completely valid. For example, as previously mentioned, functional anger can be a very effective

130

way to create boundaries and protection. The communication point could be, *you've crossed a line, now back off!* Or, for someone who is in a moment of being overcome by tears and sadness, the purpose of the comms might be to convey to you, *I'm a mess right now, hold me!* In these situations, it's obviously appropriate to just be in the emotion and let it flow.

If, however, you want the other person to understand why you feel the way you do—say, for example, you are completely frustrated and are trying to explain the cause of your frustration—there is every chance your message will be lost in the storm of the frustration itself. The person you are trying to communicate with will certainly see you are frustrated, but will likely miss any nuance beneath the waves.

Your message could be conveyed more effectively, and therefore better understood, from a place of calm centeredness—from a place of conscious awareness.

So how do we get better at that? There are ways we can improve our ability to be "the driver of our own bus." There are certain mind practices that, over time, make it easier for us to influence our physiology, our emotional, mental, and physical state. You can learn how to take yourself from being flustered to calm, from angry to equanimous, even from nervous to relaxed.

One of my favorite techniques, mindful observation, is a practice (yep, another one!), and when it becomes a way of life, it is quite a profound tool. Mindfulness itself is simply an unbiased observation of the present moment. It is a practice of noticing anything that is showing up in consciousness.

Just because it's simple, though, doesn't mean it's easy! We have very busy minds, with a continuous flow of thoughts, and are very easily distracted and carried away. The practice, however, is a training of the mind. Every time you bring your focus back to what you are observing, you strengthen the "mind muscle" needed to stay present. The objects of your attention can be anything you notice arising in the moment—sounds, sensations, emotions, even thoughts.

Over time, as we develop the ability to observe an experience rather than just be consumed by it, we gain better control over our state of being. By "stepping outside" an emotion, for example, and simply noticing how it shows up in conscious awareness, we are in a sense releasing ourselves from the grip of identifying with that internal, emotional mental looping. Without trying to "do anything" to the emotion, just in the act of careful and close, unbiased attention, the emotional state itself passes very quickly.

Similarly, with the observation of thoughts themselves, as purely objects appearing and disappearing in consciousness, with this mindfulness practice, they too can drift by with little to no consequence.

Applying this technique whilst in communication greatly assists in remaining calm, present, and focused. The experience of being listened to by someone who is completely present, undistracted, and solely focused on you is really quite exquisite. Likewise, the ability to be able to monitor and manage your internal state, whilst delivering communication, is of immense value. Imagine hardly ever losing your cool (save space for some apparently necessary irrationality), rarely having nerves get in the way of your delivery, and maintaining the clarity of mind to speak from your center of equanimity (calmness and composure)! Wow.

By the way, the benefits of developing your mind to be able to integrate this state of awareness into other activities greatly enhance and improve your experience of them. Paying closer attention to (being completely present to) tasting your favorite food, for example, elevates the experience (and apparently improves digestion). Simply being present to the experience of hitting a tennis ball, rather than thinking about hitting the tennis ball, improves your ability to hit the tennis ball. Tasting chocolate when you are not distracted explodes the experience into the realms of ecstasy. When two people are completely present in sex, not caught up in their thoughts, their experience is sublime. Mindfully listening not only improves your ability to comprehend, but the person sharing feels it, relaxes, and gains confidence, because they feel like you care, and subsequently communicates more effectively—because of the way you listened mindfully!

How to Train Mindfulness

Once again, I find simplifying something to be very effective. We can easily procrastinate on doing something by staying in "overwhelm." When it all seems too much or too big or too hard, we just put it off. The idea of incorporating meditation practice into your life can seem all too much, and the benefits too elusive, so why bother. Here's what I did to make it easier to incorporate mindfulness practices into my habitual way of being.

I like to see two forms of mindfulness practice: integrated and dedicated. Integrated mindfulness is the practice of being mindful (paying close, unbiased attention to the present moment) in the act of doing something you would ordinarily be doing anyway: brushing your teeth, driving the car, washing the dishes, etc. This is great for people who say, "I don't have time to meditate," because it doesn't take any time out of your day.

The practice is simple, though not necessarily easy! While you are doing that thing—say, for example, brushing your teeth—just keep bringing all of your attention to what you can notice in that moment: the taste of the toothpaste, the feeling of the bristles on your teeth and gums, the sound of it, etc. You will notice your thoughts sidetrack to what happened earlier that day, or what time you need to get up tomorrow morning, or what you were just watching on TV. It's okay. Just keep bringing your focus back to the place of observation, noticing the present moment.

This is the training. *This* is the practice. It's good for you, a healthy thing to do, and over time, you actually get better at staying focused. Can you imagine the positive flow-on effect for things like concentration and productivity, let alone your ability to stay present in communication with others?

That's all well and good, but you may be asking, "How do I remember to do that? How do I create a habit?" One of the most successful habit-forming hacks I've come across is to link the new habit you want to form with an existing habitual activity. This is why I use brushing teeth as an example. It's something we do daily already, hopefully twice a day. So, you take a Post-it note and write "Mindfully" on it and stick it next to your toothbrush holder. This way, every time you go to brush your teeth, you will be reminded.

What happens over time is that we create a neural association, and one action reminds us to do the other. I don't have a note in the bathroom anymore, but when I reach for my toothbrush, I am reminded to practice. I've also linked the habit of making my coffee in the morning with an integrated mindfulness practice as well. ☺

Dedicated mindfulness is just as it suggests—making some time to sit and practice mindful observation. This is typically called meditation. The benefits of a meditation practice have been widely researched and documented. You can find this literature easily online. Once again, my intention in this book is not to try and prove if and how something works, but rather to share practical ways to implement strategies that will improve your communication.

Try the dedicated mindfulness process I explain in the forthcoming paragraph and see for yourself. How do you feel immediately afterwards? Spending a few minutes doing this before any important, planned comms is immediately helpful. The long-term effect on your quality of life is something only you will understand, after some time of practice.

A Dedicated Mindfulness Process

Find somewhere to sit where you won't be interrupted. Simply sit, on either a chair or a pillow on the floor. Make sure you are comfortable enough. Close your eyes and take a few deeper, longer breaths. As you exhale, do so with a sense of letting go. Now take your attention to what you can hear. Just notice each sound, and then listen for any other sounds. Drop any stories your thoughts are attaching to the sounds. Just notice them.

Then take your attention to any physical sensations you can notice: points of contact with the chair or floor, perhaps your hands on your lap, any internal sensations. Again, drop any associated stories and simply notice the sensations.

Finally, take your attention to your breath. Don't try and change it, just notice it. Follow the inhalation right through to the exhalation. When you notice you've become distracted and carried away in your thoughts, simply bring yourself back to noticing your breath. *This* is the practice.

When you are ready, open your eyes and come back into the room. This whole process can be only a couple of minutes, or a much longer meditation. You could even put this book down now and give it a try...go on. Notice how you feel afterwards.

Creating a meditation practice isn't easy. It can just seem "not that important" and there can be a perception of not having enough time in the day for another healthy thing to do. So, here are some tips to make it easier. Two minutes of meditation is a thousand times better than none. Start by introducing something achievable. Set your alarm just two minutes early, three times a week. This is how you make a practice part of your life.

Use a guided meditation app if that makes it easier for you, or just sit quietly and notice your breath for two minutes. Maybe you prefer to do it before going to sleep at night. You might find it's a nice way to drift off to sleep.

After some time of forcing myself to meditate in the mornings, it started to become something I look forward to! It's an escape from the "doing." For me it has become a timeout from having to fix problems, or parent, or work—all the things we are so busy doing. I look forward to my twenty minutes of morning meditation, and I certainly feel more fresh and ready for the day afterwards. ☺

Over time and practice, you will notice it becomes easier for you to implement mindfulness into moments. As much as meditation teachers tell us that's not the point—we don't meditate to strive for anything—getting better at being mindful in moments just happens to be a longer-term benefit.

Becoming more conscious in communication (and in general), is a combination of learning more about the way you and others operate *and* practicing being more present and less distracted. In the chapters to come, I am going to share with you some useful models of various human behaviors.

I call them macro behavioral patterns, because they apply, in some way, to all humans. These patterns will help you understand why you behave in certain ways and why some others seem to go about things so differently. Understanding why and how we behave the way we do improves our capacity for understanding, compassion, acceptance, and communication.

Chapter Thirteen

A PROCESS

Before we start exploring human macro behavioral patterns, I would like to share a simple process for conscious communication preparation. This process obviously applies to planned comms—comms you know you will be having. It can apply to different contexts and formats of communication, whether it be a keynote speaking engagement, a one-on-one work meeting, a team meeting, a tough conversation with someone close to you, an announcement, a speech, giving feedback, motivating or inspiring, etc. If there is something you need to communicate at some point in the future and you have any time at all to prepare for it, this process will help.

Why–Who–What–How–When–Pause–Share

A functional and empowering mindset to have when approaching communication is that, if you're the one with something to say, the success of the comms is your responsibility (I would like to add here that if you are the listener, it is also a wonderful practice to seek to understand). If the communicator really cares about getting the message across, they do well to tailor their delivery to the context. After all, if the most important thing is the communication itself, then learning how to be flexible and adaptive in your delivery will only increase your chances of being understood.

STEP ONE: WHY?

The first step is to be clear on the purpose of the comms. This will help greatly in forming an effective way of going about things. This is another time for the question, "For what purpose?" Again, not only helpful in planning comms, but also in many situations when deciding whether and how to proceed with something.

The reason for the comms could be as simple as needing to share some instructions. Perhaps you're meeting a friend somewhere and you need to describe how to get there. The purpose of this communication would be so that your friend easily finds the spot. Maybe the reason for the comms is less literal; you want your partner to feel loved, or you want one of your children to feel safe. Sometimes the purpose of communicating is to establish personal boundaries to "protect" or "preserve" yourself and/or the relationship.

Sometimes the purpose could be easily lost in the heat of the moment if the conversation is at risk of being confrontational.

For example, you're giving constructive feedback to someone on a team you lead, and they have a track record of being defensive and reactionary. The purpose is not "to give feedback"; the purpose is to help the person develop and improve. Remembering this will help you aim for the best way toward that end.

First step: get clear on the purpose. Why are you having this communication?

STEP TWO: WHO?

People are different. Not only do we look different from each other, we process information in different ways as well. Some people are naturally inclined toward the "big picture" and don't have much patience for the finer points. Others feel unsettled with not enough clarity and attention to detail in the communication. Some of us are very visual and some of us are more kinesthetic—i.e., it's more to do with how we feel about something. Some people are wired to process information literally and chronologically, whereas others prefer broad-stroke, emotive narrative. Some people will make decisions on the spot, based on the information available, and others prefer a period of time to process and percolate before responding or deciding.

Some people want you to get straight to the point, and others will be offended if you don't begin with some polite chitchat. Some prefer you to say it just as it is, and then others may like a touch of emotional intelligence, some compassion and care in the delivery.

You might be thinking by now, "How on earth am I going to deliver comms the best way when there are so many variables?" Well, don't worry: in the forthcoming chapters I am going to help you understand how to read some of the "macro code" of our human matrix. I call these behaviors "macro" because they apply to all humans in some way, across age, gender, and culture. There are some basic things we all have in common to varying degrees, and this is a good place to start to understand others.

Of course, we also have what I call our own "micro-idiosyncrasies." These are the unique parts of your personality that have been formed due to all the events and stories of your beautifully intricate life. The better you know someone, the more of these you are privy to.

Humans are complex creatures, and it can take a lot of dedication and practice to read the intricate weave of a person's tapestry. It is therefore best to start with some of the more simple, shared patterns and work your way from there.

STEP THREE: WHAT?

Have you ever found yourself in the middle of what has become a heated conversation, only to forget the main points of what you were wanting to have understood? Sometimes being misconstrued can even seem to create a glitchy feedback loop, which then affects your ability to be clear, and before you know it, the whole conversation has spiraled south.

In the planning phase for your upcoming conscious communication, take a pen and some paper and jot down in dot-point form the main points of what you want to convey. If the conversation has any potential to involve emotion, take your piece of paper with you.

My suggestion is to start the comms appropriately for "who" you are communicating with (small talk and pleasantries, or not), and then let them know you've written some notes, because you want to stay on track for them.

Obviously, there are occasions where it's not going to serve the purpose of the comms to pull out a piece of paper with your points on it. Use your sensibility and be discerning. Also, if you haven't set it up the right way, pulling out notes to go through can elicit a defensive reaction from people as well. That's why I start the conversation without the list, then use it if I need to.

At the very least, simplify what it is you want to communicate, and keep it simple when explaining it. Try to remember the adage "less is more." When you are calm, clear, measured, and mindful, you stand a better chance of remaining conscious in comms.

STEP FOUR: HOW?

There are different mediums, times (see Step Five), and places to communicate. Choose the most appropriate combo for why, who, and what you want to say. Does the comms need to be documented in an email? Is it best said one-on-one, or in a group forum? Will a phone call do, or does it need to be face-to-face?

Here are some general rules of thumb:

- If the material has the potential to be taken the wrong way, go for face-to-face, or Zoom at least. If that's not possible, pick up the phone. If it's information that should be documented as well, by all means send an email, *after* you've spoken to them live.

  "Hi, I've got that feedback from the board you asked for. I'll put it in an email and send it through. Before I do, I just wanted to talk you through it to make sure you get where they're coming from."

- If the information is purely logistical, then text, email, messenger, WhatsApp—you name it, however you know they will get the info best.

- If it's constructive criticism, it's best done one-on-one.

- If it's praise or celebratory, it's fine in public.

- If it's emotional, intimate, or a matter of the heart, not only should it be face-to-face, but pick the right time as well.

STEP FIVE: WHEN

You know those times when you are in the middle of something; perhaps the task requires extra focus because it's not happening smoothly. You may even be starting to experience mild frustration, but you are determined to work it out and get it done. Then, out of nowhere, your partner calls out from the other room, asking your opinion on what seems to you a completely irrelevant (and perhaps unimportant) matter. You call back, with a slightly more irritated tone than intended, "Not now, I'm in the middle of something!" *Grrrrr*. Timing.

Timing matters. It matters a lot for a lot of things. For a fascinating and informative read on this subject, I can recommend Daniel H. Pink's book *When: The Scientific Secrets of Perfect Timing*. In this book, Daniel shares data showing judges being more (or less) strict with sentences varying with the time of day, their energy, and their hunger levels. He talks about the mistake ratios of surgeons and their teams in hospitals varying with the time of day. He shares stories of catastrophic decisions being made by people in very important roles due to the times when they made the decisions.

We have body clock cycles that affect our moods, decision-making ability, creative abilities, focus, and so on. You may get very different responses from the same person depending on where they are in their cycle and/or what other external factors are contributing to their state of mind.

You will also get very different responses from someone depending on how tired, or stressed, or emotional they are. These factors are influenced by a range of variables—some unpredictable, and some as predictable as the monthly lunar cycle. Get to know those you care about, their cycles, their timing, their rhythms.

The point of this step is, choose your timing wisely. Here are some things to consider when choosing your timing:

- When giving development feedback as a coach or leader, pertaining to a specific incident, "sooner rather than later" is the rule of thumb. (Of course, remember this should also be in the appropriate context—one to one, within the coaching relationship, etc.) There's not much point in going up to a report and saying, "I need to give you some feedback on the way you did [that thing] six months ago."

- If you have an idea you want your partner to get on board with, pick a time when their "love tank" is full— say, after you've been successfully communicating your love for them in their Love Language (see Chapter Sixteen).

- If something isn't urgent, perhaps it's better to make a note of it and bring it up at a later stage.

- If you're upset about something, try to choose a time when you are calm and not in the heat of the moment.

- If it will benefit the others involved to have some time to prepare; don't leave the communication until the last minute.

STEP SIX: PAUSE

This is the moment immediately prior to engaging in the communication. Before you walk in the door, pick up the phone, enter the virtual room, or start typing the email—pause; take a few slightly deeper, slower breaths; and take twenty or thirty seconds to do a "mindfulness scan" of where you are at.

This can be as simple as noticing what shows up in your conscious awareness—what you can hear, feel, and sense. Notice where your heartbeat is at, your breathing, your thoughts.

Just simply notice these things. You don't need to change anything. Once you have become more present, walk through the door and clearly commence your Conscious Comms!

STEP SEVEN: SHARE

I've used the word "share" here instead of "deliver" or "tell" because this suggests communication being at least a two-way flow of energy—or in the case of a team or group, or even when keynote speaking, a multi-directional sharing of energy and information.

Even if it appears that the communication only needs to be "one-way," like the giving of simple directions, conscious communication is the awareness that there is always an exchange in the dialogue through the acknowledgment that there has been an understanding. This can be overt—"Please let me know what you heard"— or implied through the more subtle signs of body language and vocal tone.

When the communication obviously needs to be flowing in both directions, remembering these few tips will certainly help.

- Put your ego to the side. The less defensive you are, the better.

- Seek to understand. The more open to other perspectives you are, the more well-rounded the solutions can be.

- Stay present. Don't queue up to speak. When you're listening, practice mindfulness and be as present as possible.

- Carefully keep it simple. Choose your words wisely. Less is more.

WHY

WHO

WHAT

HOW

WHEN

PAUSE

SHARE

Chapter Fourteen

HUMAN PATTERNS AND COMMUNICATION

Feminine and Masculine in Communication

When you read anything written on "masculine and feminine energy styles," you will undoubtedly see a similar clarification to the one in the next paragraph. It goes something like this:

When we talk about "feminine" and "masculine" energies, styles, or behaviors, it's *not* about females or males. In fact, we *all* have access to both feminine and masculine energy. Most people are naturally wired one way more than the other, a handful are reasonably balanced, but almost none of us are completely just one or the other. We can also, thanks to neuroplasticity, through environment and/or intention, change our mix of the two.

I do, however, find it incredibly useful to understand the two different aspects of "being human" in the context of communication, and hence am including this conversation in the book.

Just to be clear before we proceed, some males are more feminine than masculine, and some females vice versa. This is not about sexual orientation, nor is it about outward appearance or body language. There are heterosexual men who operate more naturally with their feminine energy, and homosexual men who are more masculine. There is every permutation of these combinations, and yep, you guessed it—every shade along the spectrum between the poles.

So, let's just leave the stereotypes aside and focus on these two different ways of communicating. People naturally move between and blend the two energy styles at any point in time. By understanding this, you may become better at perceiving how people can see more than just one opinion of any given situation.

To enable me to give examples and share stories whilst avoiding the present hot water and firing lines we can find ourselves in due to the "political incorrectness" of using traditional pronouns, I have decided to create my own. When I am referring to the masculine energy, I will use "Ta"; when referring to the feminine energy, "Ka."

Remember, as I explain this topic further in the coming paragraphs, I am not referring to particular people, and certainly not referring to any gender whatsoever. The reason I am belaboring this point is because it's very likely that, along with most others who read this book, you have been indoctrinated with gender stereotypes. It actually takes quite a determined form of mental gymnastics to leap beyond your predisposed assumptions. Ta and Ka can be either person in any relationship. And remember, individuals can (and do) move between Ta and Ka.

Ta (masculine energy style) thinks and speaks literally, logically, and linearly. Ta calls a spade a spade. Ka (feminine energy style) thinks, feels, and speaks laterally, emotionally, and circularly. Ka doesn't necessarily say what Ka means, rather insinuates. Ta is mainly focused on the result, whereas Ka is more focused on the relationship. Ta wants to get to the outcome, and Ka is more naturally in the present moment.

Let me give you a made-up example of where Ta and Ka come unstuck in miscommunication.

One day, Ka is feeling emotional and frustrated. Ka has been asking Ta for help on a job around the house that requires two people. Ta didn't think it was very important and has kept putting it off. On this particular day, Ka has had a terrible night's sleep and been lying awake all night thinking about the undone job.

The next morning, while they are quietly sitting, sipping their tea and reading the newspaper, Ka asks again, "Baby, can we please get that thing done?"

Without looking up from the paper, Ta replies, "Yeah, yeah, we can do it later."

Ka bursts out with, "Fuck, I'm *so* sick of you! You *never* do anything for me! You're so fucking *selfish*!"

Ta is snapped out of Ta's state of calm. Ta takes Ka's words literally and thinks to Ta-self, I make you *sick*? I *never* do *anything* for you? *I'm* selfish???!!! What the fuck?! and then, defensively and angrily, Ta's ego blurts back:

"You are *so* fucking unappreciative! All the things I do for you, and you say I do *nothing*! What planet are you on? One minute you're fine, sipping tea, the next minute you're fucking crazy mad at me! I can't keep up with you, Ka!"

Then Ta marches off thinking to "give Ka some space" but really to get away and escape the storm.

What Ta didn't understand is that Ka was expressing the emotion Ka was feeling in that moment. Ka didn't literally mean "sick" or "never," Ka meant, "Aaaarrrghhh, I'm fucking exhausted and frustrated, and you don't understand what's important to me. You're not seeing me right now and showing me you love me and care about me by helping me do that one thing. Gggrrrrrrrahhhhhhh."

Ta didn't actually need to take it personally or literally. Ta just needed to sit still and listen, validate Ka's emotional expression, and honor the powerful feminine energy—remember each person in this scenario can be *any* gender.

When Ka felt heard, validated, understood, and loved (and when the nagging job was done), Ka might easily move through a range of emotions from frustration and anger to forgiveness, gratitude, and love. Within a very short space of time, Ka might even then nestle into Ta's arms and say, "I'm sorry, baby, I didn't mean those things I said, I'm just so tired."

"All good, my love. I didn't realize how much you wanted that thing done. I love you and I want to get better at understanding."

Another common snag the masculine and feminine often trip up on is Ta's natural tendency to jump to the end point (result-focused) of what Ka is saying and then try to "fix" the problem. If you are in your masculine and trying to listen to your partner in feminine telling you something, you may find yourself thinking, "Yeah, yeah, I get it, baby, get to the point." In the meantime, your partner is telling you the same thing in five different ways over and over. This can be frustrating, and you may even want to cut them off by saying, "Honey, I get it. Just move A to B and then you won't have to deal with C anymore! Problem solved."

Essentially, you've just inadvertently shut Ka down and potentially misunderstood the purpose of the comms. Ka was more likely wanting to communicate how Ka was feeling, taking some time to use different words to express Ka-self, get it off Ka's chest, and feel heard. Now Ka thinks, "Ta doesn't get me, Ta cuts me off, Ta doesn't really care." Whereas Ta was just trying to help by fixing Ka's problem. Innocent misunderstanding and miscommunication on both sides, leaving Ta feeling irritated and Ka feeling unloved.

Oh, and by the way, sometimes Ka *is* just wanting Ta to fix something. It can be confusing and sometimes hard to gauge. I find it helpful to just ask, if I'm not sure.

No one taught us this stuff in school! Imagine if this kind of content were a high school subject—Advanced Interpersonal Communication. Now there's an idea. ☺

The bottom line is, we need the full spectrum of energies ranging from what has become known as "masculine" through to "feminine," not just in communication, but also in life. As we need the moon and the sun, day and night, summer and winter, yin and yang, this model is another example of AD (apparent duality). The two complements coexist and blend. We can be both at the same time. However, I think it's helpful to understand the poles of this spectrum, to become more conscious and adaptive in communication.

Feminine is our creative, intuitive, moving, dancing life force. Masculine is our planning, goal-achieving, process-following, and action-taking aspects. Ta takes action and rushes in to do what needs to be done. Ka is our access to the broader scope of emotions, being alive in the present moment. Ta is the knowledge. Ka is the knowing.

In earlier days, my journey of discovering these different energies within was mostly confusing. I've always had easy access to both feminine and masculine energies. I identified as a "creative" through my teens and twenties. This was the time in my life when my teenage sweetheart told me I "didn't feel like a man for her."

My role-modelling of masculine from my father was both functional and dysfunctional (AD). There were aspects of him as "a man" that upset me deeply and drove my rebellion. For example, the way he disciplined me through fear and a very patriarchal "dominance" structure. Two sharp, loud claps of his hands from the other end of the house, and I would stop in my tracks and pray there were no smacks coming. He also had ways I idolized and to this day admire: his desire and actions to provide the best possible life for Mum and us kids. His remarkable work ethic and leadership. The way he would decisively book us a trip around the world, or the next camping adventure. It's really only with the understanding I have now that I can look back and make sense of the behaviors I abhorred and rebelled against, as well as those I respected and tried to emulate.

I initially couldn't comprehend what it meant to "be a man," because our cultural stereotypes didn't work for me; however, I latched on to one of the most common masculine archetypes when I became a father, that of Provider. It felt good to take on responsibility, earn money, pay the bills, put a roof over my family's head and food in the fridge. I thought that was all I had to do.

That alone, unfortunately, didn't amount to understanding my then-wife when she was in her feminine. Or when she was accessing her masculine. Our miscommunications became plenty, and the disappointment of being unable to reconcile slowly dried things up until the drought became a desert.

It's only been in my current relationship, after studying and practicing these understandings, that I have been able to really explore my functional masculine and honor my partner's powerful, functional feminine. Rather than retreating from "noise" to escape, I now practice staying present, leaning in (so to speak), finding my grounded stillness, peace, and quiet within, and making myself completely available to her; seeking to understand. I've learnt now that Provider is only a part of my masculine access. Action-taker, Decision-Maker, Mission-Focused, Planner, Listener, Steadier, Enabler, and Make-Shit-Happen-Man are also archetypes that I'm practicing and are working well for me.

My partner also has very easy access to her masculine energy. She runs her own businesses and loves getting results. When she is in her masculine, she gets to the point and has a laser focus. She calls things straight, no fluff, no bullshit. She sets a goal and makes it happen.

It's actually fun for us both to be aware of which energy style the other is in at any given time, and we can then communicate accordingly.

When one partner is in their masculine and the other is in their feminine, the charge of attraction is possible. Another fun part of the Game of Life. ☺

SOME COMMUNICATION STRATEGIES

Communicating with someone who's in their masculine:

- Get straight to the point

- Proceed in a logical and linear manner

- Let them know you appreciate the things they do

- Speak literally

- Allow some space for peace and quiet

Communicating with someone who's in their feminine:

- Seek to understand

- Don't take words literally

- Let the conversation meander and evolve

- Allow time to talk through things

- Don't try and jump to the end

- Don't try and "fix" them or their problems

If you are interested in reading more deeply into this topic, I recommend David Deida's books, particularly *The Way of the Superior Man*. Both my partner and I got a lot from this book.

The second time through, we read it to each other, taking turns chapter for chapter. We do this with other personal development books as well. Not only is this quality time together (see Chapter Sixteen), but when your loved one is on a similar trajectory of growth, when you are sharing content and ideas that inspire, you are both much more likely to adopt the learnings and evolve in an aligned way.[5*]

---

5 * A note to keep in mind: Functional and dysfunctional play into this Ta/Ka conversation as well. Practice being mindful of where you are on the scale.

Chapter Fifteen

THE FOUR BEHAVIORAL/ COMMUNICATION STYLES

Back in my days of believing I wasn't good enough, my natural way of getting things done around the house was a source of irritation for my then-wife, and subsequently more evidence to me that I wasn't enough. I'd be in the middle of folding clothes to put away, then notice that dripping laundry tap and go on a fix-it tangent, maybe come back to the washing via answering a work text, and then, when delivering clothes to the kids' rooms, go on another tangent to tidy their toys.

"Just finish what you're doing before you go on to the next thing!"

Then, when I studied the behavioral styles I'm going to share with you here, I realized, "There's other people like me! And we all have shiny-thing-distraction-syndrome!"

When we separated and I started living on my own (with the kids week on, week off), I could just relax and do the housework in my seemingly random, distracted, multitasking fashion. I started saying to myself, *As long as you're doing something that needs to be done around the house, Jem, then it's all getting done and will be finished in the same amount of time. Just keep going.*

We like to think that we are all very individual and unique. And yes, in some ways we are. But in a lot of ways, we are incredibly predictable and fit within certain patterns of behavior. When someone is behaviorally very similar to you, it's easier to get along. You both just seem to "get each other." When someone is different to you, it's quite often trickier to get into a flow with each other.

Have you ever met someone and thought, *Wow, you are so abrupt, so frank! No sugar-coating going on there!* Or perhaps you've come across people and thought, *Oh my God, get to the point! What are you trying to say? Stop fluffing around.*

Maybe there have been people you just don't understand at all. How on earth did they come to that conclusion or make that decision?

Have there been times when you were sure you communicated something clearly, only to find that it was completely misinterpreted?

More often than not, these situations have something to do with differing behavioral styles. In this chapter, I'm going to explain and put into the context of Conscious Communication the fascinating and well-established understanding of four distinctive human styles. This work appeared in literature as early as 400 BC, with the physician Hippocrates outlining "four temperaments."

In 1921, Dr. Carl Jung, a Swiss psychiatrist, psychoanalyst, and the founder of modern psychology, published his book *Psychological Types*, in which he delineated four distinct aspects of the human psyche. This work was the foundation for later psychologists and philosophers to continue research and understanding in this area. One of them, Dr. William Marston, in his book *Emotions of Normal People*, elaborated on these four styles in DISC theory.

It is in the understanding of these four types as "behavioral styles" that we will here explore communication preferences and strategies. It's important to note that we are not talking about personalities. Your personality is more unique and "fixed" than generic behaviors. We can (and do) shift our behavioral styles contextually, and quickly if need be. However, we tend to have a preferred, or "lead" style that is our default. We can access the behaviors of our non-preferred styles, if need be—it just takes more energy to do so.

There are no right or wrong styles. We usually are a blend of a few. No one is completely balanced across all four. Some are very much oriented in only one. In each of the four styles, there are functional and dysfunctional manifestations. This can also be understood as well-adjusted or not-so-well-adjusted individuals. Remember the AD spectrum? There is every gradient in between functional and dysfunctional, and we can move along or jump quickly from one place to another on this scale.

I'll start by broadly describing each style, and then we can explore communication strategies for them.

RESULTS

INTROVERT, DETAIL		EXTROVERT, BIG PICTURE
CONSCIENTIOUS COMPLIANT precise facts logical hates mistakes non-emotional		**DOMINANT DECISIVE** get to the point assertive fast-paced wants to win controlling
WHAT IF	WHAT	
HOW	WHO	
STEADFAST STABILITY security resists change process people team player emotional		**INFLUENCER INTERACTIVE** friendly rapport easily distracted let's make it fun connected emotional

RELATIONSHIP

Let's begin with the most intense energy of the four: *D*. Dominant, Decisive, Direct. You know when these people are in the room. They love to be in control. They come across as confident and self-assured. *D*s are driven by the need to win. Their archetype is the Warrior. They love the battle. *D* is a masculine energy style, result- and goal-focused. Remember from the previous chapter on masculine and feminine that this doesn't mean D-style people are males; there are female *D*s as well. They are big-picture people and get impatient with too much detail or dragging of the heels. They make decisions quickly and they love change. "If it ain't broke, break it, build it bigger, better, faster, stronger."

*D*s are extroverts; they get charged by being out and about, making things happen. They are "future-assurance-based"; they base their trust or judgement on how they think something will impact them moving forward. They are quite often mainly concerned with themselves, or their agenda.

They are results-focused and can be known for inadvertently upsetting people in their blunt, no-bullshit communication. Preserving the relationship with niceties or emotional intelligence is just not in the forefront of their wiring. Not to say they can't do this; it would just take energy to do so.

Functional *D*s make strong leaders and visionaries, quite often the CEO or entrepreneur. Dysfunctional *D*s can be aggressive bullies, intimidating and controlling.

Their communication style is direct and assertive. Get to the point. Not too much detail. Wanting to feel in control. Enjoy the battle with *D*s; they respect fact-based arguments. Don't take it personally when they are abrupt. It's not about you.

Next are our *I*-style people. Influencer, Interactive, Inspiring. This style is also extrovert, big-picture and future-assurance-based, with not much interest in the detail at all. *I*s are driven by the need to be liked and for everyone to get along. A feminine energy style, they are more focused on the relationship than the result.

*I*s can get along with just about anyone, and they are authentically chameleon, adapting and adjusting to fit into any scene. One of their top core values is "fun." "If we're not having fun, what's the point?" they say. Their archetype is the Joker. They are happy to be the life of the party and entertain the group.

*I*s are easily distracted; one might say they have "shiny-thing-distraction-syndrome." Notifications on a smart phone are an irresistible distraction, leading them down mines of rabbit holes. The intention to pick up the device and email a colleague can often result in searching for a new pair of jeans on Pinterest via every other social media and comms platform along the way. "What was I doing again?" they ask.

Functional versions of this behavioral style can bring groups of people together and inspire them to a common cause. They can sell ideas and help others see the silver lining. Diehard optimists.

Dysfunctions of the *I* include over-promising, missing important details, and sometimes getting too swept up in their emotions.

For *I*s in communication, it's about rapport and connection. They want everyone to get along, and will choose their words accordingly. The last thing they want to do is offend anyone. *I*s will notice your haircut or new suit and compliment you on it. They will point out your strengths and try to make you feel good.

When communicating with an *I*, schedule time for chitchat. Ask them how their weekend was or how their family is. Find something you have in common and use it as a talking point.

The *S* in DISC stands for Steadfast, Stability, Submissive. This behavioral style is introvert, detail-oriented, and "past-assurance-based." They will look back on the history of something to help them evaluate it. The archetype for *S* is the Mother. No, that doesn't just mean females. There are males with this as their lead style as well. It just means the Nurturer, the Carer.

Our *S*s are driven by the need for security, and they resist change, especially if they feel it is unnecessary. "If it ain't broke, don't fix it, just leave it, it's working fine." They don't seek to be in charge, and prefer to be a part of the team. They are very loyal.

As with the *I*-style, the feminine energy *S* is more focused on maintaining the relationship. They are wonderful team players and very loyal. They prefer a steady pace and to not be rushed. *S*s prefer time to make a decision, considering the details and track record of something first.

If you come into a team meeting and there is a jug of water in the middle of the table, *S*s will ask everyone if they would like some. *D*s, on the other hand, will just come in, fill their own glass, and then announce to the room, "Right, c'mon, let's get on with it! This is what we are doing!"

Functional *S*s think of everyone and everything, making sure all is okay. Dysfunctional *S*s can get stuck with indecision, not tell you how they're really feeling, and dig their heels in to resist change (change = uncertainty = lack of security).

When communicating with an *S*, slow down. Schedule enough time to go through the detail systematically, with less sense of urgency.

Last but by no means least, we come to our Professor archetype, *C*. Conscientious. Compliant. Cautious. These are our thinkers, very much in their head. Ask a *C* how they feel about something, and that doesn't quite compute. "What do you mean? I don't feel anything, it just doesn't make sense." Also introvert, detail-focused, and past-assurance-based like *S*, but the masculine version of these shared traits. *C*-style people are driven by the need for things to be correct, to be accurate and precise. They operate logically and follow the rules. "If you are going to do something, you should do it properly."

Ask a *C* what time it is, and they will tell you exactly, "It's one fifty-six." Ask an *I* the same thing and they will say, "About two-ish."

When a *C* brings home a DIY furniture flat pack, they open the packaging neatly and methodically and go first to the instructions. They will go through all the nuts and bolts and make sure everything is there. Then they will construct the new bookshelf systematically and exactly. Our *I*s, on the other hand, will excitedly rip the packaging open and jump straight into building—maybe getting stuck halfway through and saying, "Where are those instructions?" They may even have a couple of leftover screws at the end and tell you they are "spares."

Functional *C*s are great critical thinkers and risk mitigators. They can adopt new ways of thinking immediately if the new way makes more sense. Dysfunctional *C*s can be perpetual non-decision-makers because they hate making mistakes so much.

Let's now look at some other differences between the styles.

- For *D*s, it's all about the "what." "What's your point?" "What's the meeting for?" "What's the movie about?"

- For *I*s, it's more about "who." "Who is coming to the meeting?" "Who's in the movie?" "Who's going to be at the party?"

- *S*s are more interested in "how." "How are we going to get everyone to the meeting?" "How are we going to get to the movies? Your car is being serviced, the babysitter is away on holidays," etc. (thinking of the details).

- *C*s are focused on "what if." "What if COVID-19 restrictions come again and prevent the meeting?" "What if your car breaks down?" "What if the finance falls through?" and so on.

The older of my two teenage boys's lead behavioral style is *C* (with a lot of *S*). The other is a strong *D*. They are like chalk and cheese. Before I knew anything about the four behavioral styles, I would quite often wonder, "Where did these little people come from?!" They are *so* different in many ways from each other and from me and their mum.

When my older boy asked what the time is, "two-ish" wouldn't suffice. "No, Dad, what exactly is the time?" When my younger boy (driven by the need to win) was losing at a board game, he would crack it, throw down his cards, and storm out, saying, "This game is dumb! I'm not playing a stupid game!"

Of course, my children (and all of us) are way more intricate and complex than just their behavioral styles, but this human macro pattern certainly is a useful tool to help us deliver our communication more effectively.

Another difference between the styles is in our decision-making strategies:

- *D*s are what we call an "automatic convincer with criteria." This means they make decisions on the spot, with the relevant dot-points. Don't give them too much detail, just enough so they feel informed enough to make a winning decision.

- *I*s are also an "automatic convincer," but with no criteria! They will make a decision on the spot, without even looking at any detail. In fact, they will make the decision based on whether they like you or not. Or whether it sounds like fun. They will tell you it's a "gut feel," or "intuition."

- *S*s are what we call a "period of time convincer." They prefer not to be rushed into decisions. The bigger the decision, the more time they prefer. If you try and rush them into a decision, they don't like it at all.

- *C*s are "a number of times convincer." They won't decide on the first or second pass. They will have lots of "what if" questions. If they are well-adjusted, they might decide the third time around. If not, they can be perpetual non-decision-makers. I've lost count of the number of times my older boy stands stressed in a moment of "not knowing whether to come or stay" because of not wanting to make the wrong decision!

Knowing someone's decision-making strategy greatly assists in your communication with them. If you know someone prefers some time, pressuring them to "hurry up" only causes tension, which can spill out in different ways. During the writing of this book, I said yes to coaching a new couple who were both wanting to improve as partners for their burgeoning relationship. Of course, as for so many, they kept tripping over into disharmony due to miscommunication. The bottom line is, they love each other. They both want the other to be as happy in life as possible. But they didn't get each other's behaviors. "Why does he do that?" "Why does she react like that?"

In one of our sessions, I shared with them the four behavioral styles. Talk about "penny drop moments!" He happens to be very much *D* and she is predominantly *S* (opposites attract, huh). He had been getting frustrated at her taking so long to decide on things, and she was annoyed that he would race into things without checking the details first.

One of the examples they gave me was to do with engaging a plumber to come and fix the shower. The *S* partner had been undecided for weeks on which quote to go with. The *D* partner eventually stepped in, made a decision, grabbed the phone, called the plumber, and had them coming over to do the job in twenty minutes. *S* partner worries, "But did you ask them about this? And what about that? And how are we supposed to...?" etc. She was thinking of all the details, and he was just taking big-picture action and "making shit happen." He reacted defensively to her asking about details. His ego was feeling questioned, like he wasn't good enough. "I got a result! What more do you want?"

They didn't understand behavioral styles. He just thought she was frustrating and couldn't make things happen. She just thought he was careless and would rush into things inconsiderately. After the session, they began to understand that they are just wired differently, and that's okay. They came to realize that they can actually be a great team. Together, combining their natural abilities, they can be a dynamic duo! He can respect and honor her ability to think of the important stuff he misses. She can respect and honor his ability to take action and get things done.

The more we understand someone, the greater our capacity for compassion. Compassion is a key to Conscious Communication.

You will notice behavioral styles playing out in the workplace as well. Several years ago, I was coaching the senior nurse of a large private hospital. The context of our work together was her leadership development. In one conversation, she was explaining to me the "horrible" dynamic between the nurses and the doctors. She generalized and told me how the nurses really didn't like the doctors because, "They have no bedside manner. They speak so rudely to us."

We explored the behavioral styles. She came to see that most of the nurses had a lead style of S—mother, nurturer, carer. "Of course! So that's why they were drawn to nursing in the first place!" she exclaimed. The doctors, on the other hand, were predominantly D, or D blended with C. Their focus when communicating wasn't to nurture the relationship with the nurses. It was on the decisions and actions required to get the result—saving the patient's life. They probably weren't even aware their manner was offensive. That's just not where their heads are at.

This is not to say the nurses weren't there to "get a result" too, just that their means to this same end involved maintaining the relationship with emotional intelligence, considering others' feelings, and communicating with care.

~~~~~

It's funny—after I explained the four styles to my kids, they then wanted to use their styles as an excuse for their behavior. "I can't pay attention to detail, Dad. You told me it's not part of my behavioral style!" Or, "I need to be pedantic and precise, Dad, it's just the way I am." This led to conversations on adaptability and behavioral flexibility. "Just because it's your lead style, son, doesn't mean you can't access other behaviors—it just means you need to apply yourself a bit more to them."

A teacher and mentor of mine once said, "The person with the broadest range of behavioral flexibility designs the outcome." For me this also means, "will be the most skilled (or successful) communicator." The more you can adjust your delivery to suit the person you're communicating with, the more likely you are to not only be understood, but to build deeper rapport, trust, and connection.

And yes, you can do this whilst maintaining your authenticity. You don't need to pretend to be anyone else. You can still be you whether you are "getting to the point," or "spending time asking about their weekend." If you find yourself saying, "Yeah, but I'm not interested in that stuff," or "Yeah, but I think it's important to go through all the detail," etc., you are just making it all about you. Remember, we are talking about effective communication here. Make the success of the comms the most important thing, and do what you need to do to best ensure this.

How to Know Someone's Style

Now that you have a basic understanding of the four styles, and remembering that we are usually a blend of two or three of them, I want to help you begin to pick up on people's preferred or lead style.

The easiest way is to ask. If it's someone you know well enough, I would just say to them, "Hey, I'm working on improving my ability to communicate. It would help me if I understood you a bit more. Do you mind if I ask you a few questions?" If it's not with someone where you feel comfortable to ask, then you get to have fun playing a game of behavioral sleuth!

Start with the bigger shared traits, for example, extrovert or introvert, big picture or detail, masculine or feminine, results or relationships. To help you with this, here are some general and reasonably obvious signs.

1. Do they speak up often in groups? Extrovert

2. Do they speak and act quite quickly? Extrovert

3. Are they more quiet and less likely to speak up? Introvert

4. Do they seem more measured and slower-paced? Introvert

5. Are they blunt and to the point? Masculine

6. Do they prioritize the result over people? Masculine

7. Do they consider the way they say things? Feminine

8. Are they more outwardly emotional? Feminine

If you notice someone is usually outspoken and quite blunt, you've got yourself a *D*. Or perhaps you're with someone who is talkative and really friendly, an *I*. Is the person you're observing more reserved and caring (thinks of others)? Probably an *S*. Or if you are noticing a person who is quite matter-of-fact, likes to do things right, and focuses on the details, their lead style is *C*. Just by these few observations, you now know a *whole* lot more about how the person receives, processes, and delivers information!

You know how they make decisions, what's important to them, how much time to give them, how much detail to go into with them, and whether to allocate time to chitchat, or jump straight to the point. Your ability to communicate with them potentially just went through the roof!

I know, yes, initially easier said than done, but certainly doable and gets easier with practice. The biggest challenge at the start is having the confidence to give it a go.

I should also add a footnote of sorts here: sometimes people may be in the middle of the spectrum of the bigger traits. They may be almost equally extrovert and introvert. They could possibly have equal access to masculine and feminine. It's not always straightforward. However, in my years of coaching, I've unpacked hundreds of profiles for clients and looked at many more. I've never seen a profile that is an even spread of all four styles, and I've never seen anyone have two exactly equal lead styles (although some are close).

If you're game to start having a play, you could start with friends or family members. See if you can guess, and then ask them if they prefer things the way their style would suggest. You might surprise yourself with how well you understand others now.

When I first learnt this stuff in-depth, I remember feeling excited and nervous to "try it out" with people. My first taxi ride was with a lovely Pakistani man who was super chit-chatty right from the start. Extrovert, I thought. He was smiling and making conversation with me, building the relationship. Feminine energy, I thought. Lead style *I*, I wondered. So, I had a punt.

"You like connecting with people, huh?" (an easy first guess)

"Yes, *ji*, I love people."

"You trust your intuition and make decisions quickly, yes?"

"Oh my God, how did you know that?"

"You get easily distracted, don't you?"

"Oh wow, do you have a camera in my house? My wife is always telling me I never finish the thing I am doing before I am doing several other things!"

"One of the most important things in life is to have fun, yes?"

"Yes, *ji*, of course! It is the meaning of life! Oh my God, this is uncanny! How do you know me so well, we've only just met!"

I was hooked. At the time, starting to unlock different codes of human behavior was like beginning to understand the matrix behind the way we work. Over the years of deepening this practice and combining it with knowing other macro patterns, like Core Needs, Fundamental Fears, Ego, Love Languages, and so on, it became clearer that Conscious Communication is an art and a craft that can continually be developed.

Chapter Sixteen

SHOW ME YOU LOVE ME

I won't spend too much time going into the five love languages in detail, because you can go and read Gary Chapman's books and dive deeply into his ideas there. The reason I am giving an overview here is to share how I've applied Gary's model to my life and the massive difference it has made.

The idea is that people communicate love (express love and feel loved) in different ways. Initially, Gary developed this model in the context of partners in intimate relationships, but then he extended it to all relationships: parents, children, leaders, teams, and so on. "Love" being transferable with "care."

Over his years of counselling thousands of couples, Gary identified five "languages" or ways of communicating: (1) acts of service, (2) words of affirmation, (3) gifts, (4) quality time, and (5) physical touch. We tend to have a primary and secondary language naturally, and I've experienced becoming fluent in a "language" I didn't know how to consciously converse in before.

For people whose language is acts of service, they will show you they love you by doing something for you. Likewise, they feel loved when you do something for them. They may be likely to say something like, "Words are cheap, show me that you care," or, "Actions speak louder than words." Whereas people who love in the language of words of affirmation will tell you straight up, "I love you. You are the most amazing, beautiful, thoughtful man I've ever met." For them, words mean everything. If you don't tell them you love them, they don't feel loved.

For people who communicate with gifts, it's not necessarily the money they have or haven't spent, it's the thought that counts. They will communicate that they love you by giving you gifts whenever they have the opportunity. Whereas for our quality-time people, a present doesn't mean much compared to some actual dedicated time together.

You can easily pick your friends/family/partners whose language is physical touch. Holding hands, up close on the couch watching TV, big warm greeting hugs every time, and so on. This love language is not to be confused with sex—it's just about the contact.

Once my partner and I read Gary's book, did the online test to confirm our top two languages, and then began to learn how to speak each other's language, communicating our love became even easier.

My top two languages are physical touch and words of affirmation. My partner's are acts of service and physical touch (thankfully we have that in common). Before we knew this, I would communicate my love for her by saying, "I love you. You're beautiful." But to her, those were just words. Once I knew she spoke in acts of service, I would start doing extra things for her to communicate my love. And it worked! I would look for something extra I could do as an act of service, and her love-tank would fill!

This works both ways. Now that my partner knows I communicate with words of affirmation, when she wants me to feel loved, she comes to me, looks me in the eyes, and then puts her love into words. This wasn't natural for her (it's becoming easier), and even when I know she's doing it consciously, it still works! When she stands in front of me and speaks my language, my love-tank fills.

Luckily, we are both fluent in physical touch, and still hold hands and snuggle on the couch all these years later.

One of the fringe benefits for me is that doing something that in the past would have been a chore, when it's now consciously communicating love as an act of service, has become a wonderfully enjoyable task to do. Who would've thought I would get so much pleasure from vacuuming floors, cleaning the kitchen, or running errands!

We've also been able to extend this to our four kids. By knowing what each one's love language is, we can more effectively communicate our love and care to them too.

Learning how to communicate love or care in the other person's language is certainly a skill that can be applied to the art of Conscious Communication.

Part IV

PAYING IT FORWARD

Chapter Seventeen

WEAVING IT ALL TOGETHER

A s I was writing this book and forming the flow of chapters, it became apparent that the journey on these pages is analogous to my journey of learning how to communicate through life.

About Me—About Others— Tools—Practice—Share

Who am I? How do I fit or misfit? How do I communicate that? I've experienced many quests around the world to find the answers. Relationships and stumbling through years of attempting to communicate, trying to figure out how others communicate. Midlife crisis/opportunity/reidentification. Learning tools to rebuild and more quests to practice. Live the learnings and hone the skills. Assimilate. Share.

This adventure has obviously been through the lens of being male, a male with natural access to both feminine and masculine energy in a cultural landscape where traditionally that was discouraged. A landscape still riddled with plenty of examples of dysfunctional masculine energy driving behavior.

My father was a product of his environment too. Working-class Leeds, brought up by a dad who'd survived some very close calls in battles of World War II and then post-war financial hardship. No time to be weak!

Understandably, my dad would get angry at me for being "soft" as a young boy and "too emotional." He only wanted the best for me, I'm sure. He just didn't know how to communicate that, or what that actually looked like. The two emotions Dad would allow himself to express were fun/light/irreverent, or angry.

If music evoked any deeper emotions, it was switched off. If conversations ventured away from trivial or joyful, they were shut down. If I walked through the room displaying anything that looked like a moody, brooding teenager, he would clap his hands twice and bark the order "Smile!"

The façade of "everything's okay" ended up infiltrating his life in all manner of ways, tragically becoming so twisted and hidden as to cause a brain tumor and his final departure.

Looking back now, I probably first started to create "my island" in my childhood years. I didn't feel I could communicate with Dad about all the sense-making-questions I had tumbling around in my head. I certainly couldn't talk to him about the weed I was smoking or the anxieties I was learning to bury. I had to try and hide my emotions from him, unless of course they were happy, fun, or light.

On the upside, I got lucky with the love languages. I reckon coincidentally, ours were the same; words of affirmation and physical contact. My dad told us all every day he loved us, and we would line up as kids when he got home from work every night to kiss him, hug him, and welcome him home. Yes, think the Von Trapp family from *The Sound of Music*! Suffice it to say, I always felt loved despite feeling misunderstood.

The father-son relationship was one of my first visceral experiences of AD too. I was scared of my dad, and when he smacked me and sent me to my room, I would sit on my bed cursing him. Then, every time, he would come to my room, sit lovingly by my side and win me back all over again. I loved him. He was a wonderful, funny, giving, caring man...and a pretty messed-up, self-indulgent, and confusing dude at the same time—both functional and dysfunctional on a daily basis. Ahhhh, AD, you trusty constant, there at every turn.

As a teenager, my very normal human quest to build a sense of identity, to nurture and curate my ego, to "pave my own way" was the driver for me to rebel. "Antiestablishment" was one of my favorite words. Piercings, tattoos, rock music, drugs, and dance parties—this was my church. It became successfully self-destructive. It was also the pathway to that first identity crisis in London and subsequent barefoot subcontinent quest. Conscious and intentional self-development was just around the corner.

Our access to communication with our environment—people and life around us—is interwoven with our communication with self. This has been another quite remarkable and very enjoyable benefit to come from the last eight years of practicing self-acceptance and liberating myself from negative attachments to stories from the past. The more okay I am with myself, the less it needs to be about me. This means the clearer I can see you, the more present I can be with you in communication.

Some sense of a spiritual aspect to life had always kinda been there. I was brought up in a practicing Christian family, both Catholic and Uniting Church, so a sense of mystery and something mystical was a Sunday ritual. Even after announcing to Mum and Dad when I was sixteen that I wasn't going to church anymore, I was left with a curiosity for that which can't be explained.

"Why don't you want to be Christian, Jem?" Mum asked. (This is one of the conversations I could have with her that Dad wouldn't go near!)

"Well, millions of Buddhists and Muslims and Jews and Jains and 'heathens' can't all be wrong and off to hell, Mum!"

Then, through my twenties (and ever since), with the help of my contemplative years moving through Asia, I spent plenty of time pondering the great mysteries. The undeniable perspectives that put me right there in the mix of a *massive* universe of a quantum reality we *still* can't explain the workings of. So, then, to figure out how, as a tiny part of something bigger, do we communicate with others, with life itself?

Bring in the cold hard bite again of the stuff that really hurts—death and grief. Those inevitable slaps in the face and the potential life learnings the sting can provide. How the communication of these deepest experiences can bring us closer together and to wholehearted living. Figuring out that the toughest communications, when conducted consciously, can be the most meaningful and formative.

Another teaching from the tough stuff is that we *all* have access to a range of emotions. I reckon, given half a chance and the right environment, men are open to investigating, experiencing, and communicating their own version of emotions. When we break free from the outdated and increasingly less relevant paradigm of the past, we can play our part in the inevitable evolution that's taking place. This doesn't mean we can't also be strong and steady; we can be both. We are a blend of the poles of AD.

So, as we move through the process of self-acceptance and the reparation of our relationship with the past, we begin to be able to "let go" more and more. With less to defend, conceptually, ideologically, and personally, we are able to relax our tight grip on the way we think things should be, and be open to the much broader spectrum of possibility in communication.

We become better listeners, better enablers, better lovers and leaders. Better fathers, brothers, and sons. We become better men. Remembering "letting go" doesn't mean giving up, or not guiding your family's ship through the storm. Letting go means being open to other ways of safely delivering your children over the waves.

~~~~~

Then our quest requires the acquisition of tools: understandings, strategies, practices that empower us to be better equipped for our adventure. Enter stage left—Mindfulness. Through various chapters of my life, I had dallied with Mindfulness and other forms of meditation, but mainly only as a concept about which I was curious.

It wasn't until my 2013 midlife-awakening that I began to incorporate a regular practice, both dedicated and integrated, into my life. And wow, what a game-changer it has been. Coupled with a daily practice of self-acceptance and self-love, cultivating the ability to pause in any given moment and come into my "center of steadiness" has become invaluable.

Not only has my ability to communicate enjoyed the benefits, I now have a way to make ordinary moments extraordinary. Even something as simple as drinking water, when done mindfully, can become an exquisite experience. Not to mention sipping wine, tasting delicious food, feeling the sun or breeze on your skin, or the hot water of a shower on a cold morning!

The most empowering application of Mindfulness, for me, given my experience for a time of sexual anxiety, has been in lovemaking. The ability to "get out of my head" and become completely present to my partner and the pleasure we are creating in that moment, has elevated sex beyond just "making love" to the realms of tantric and spiritual ecstasy.

Advanced learnings and the forming of an art of conscious communication really kicks into gear with the introduction of the layers of macro human behavioral patterns. I remember feeling overwhelmed at the school I attended to learn this stuff. How am I ever going to be able to take this all in, assimilate it, and become natural in the application of it? Patience, Practice, and Time, my teacher assured me.

My suggestion to you, after reading all this, would be to focus on learning one pattern at a time. For example, spend some time getting acquainted, understanding and reading people's DISC style. Remember this doesn't sum them up or pigeonhole them. It simply gives an indication of the behavioral traits which come more easily to them. It gives you an idea of their preferences.

Once you've become more practiced with that, spend some time focused on the five love languages. Then spend some time noticing Ego. After that, you could read some more on masculine and feminine energy styles, and so on. There is no "right" order to do this, just follow your curiosity.

When you feel more comfortable with these patterns in isolation, start playing with how they weave together. You may feel safer exploring the combinations of someone close to you.

As you bring all of this more into your awareness, you will notice over time that you start to read yourself and other people more naturally. Use your new power of perception to craft your communication more consciously. Make some effort to honor other people's ways, and enjoy the benefits of your upgraded comms ability!

Note

The progression through the sequences described in this book should not be only linear. Once the elements of Self, Others, Tools, and Teach have been experienced, they become coexistent and all contemporary. This is to say that a practice of self-development, awareness of others, tools, and paying it forward, all become concurrent for you.

This is the "weaving it all together." This is the true art of Conscious Communication.

Chapter Eighteen

BECOME THE TEACHER

They say the first step to learning something is when you experience it for the first time—hearing it, reading it, seeing it. The second step is when you practice it, but you only really "get" something when you teach it.

I have experienced this to be true. In fact, I've found that, in combination with practicing, the repetitive sharing or teaching of the learning continues to embed the wisdom more deeply each time.

In all my years of traveling around India, I never felt moved to follow a guru. I've met plenty of people who do, and when that works, awesome; learn and grow through the teachings and experiences of your guru. But that's just not for me. I always felt one person's sharing of life's wisdom is limited to their interpretation.

I have preferred to find teachers in all manner of situations and people. This can be in the literal sense of someone running a course I've signed up to, right through to the low-caste mum next to me on the train in the night with her three toddlers. We are all inadvertently teachers, even when we are not trying to be.

In the structured context of an organization, I love to encourage people with strategies for how to teach or lead "up the line." Going to your manager or the person you report to and saying, "Hey, you know how you were talking about what you're hoping we can achieve? Well, I've come across some cool stuff that might help us. I'd love to share with you. I think you'd really get it," is an act of service, creating an opportunity for your leader to learn, develop, evolve, and grow. They either will or won't be open to it, but if you read them well, and deliver the communication consciously, there's a chance you might help them too.

There is a fine line to be careful of, though. On one side is the generosity of sharing helpful insights with those who are interested, and on the other side is the evangelist. You know which side it's best to be on! Anyone trying to teach (convert) others when it's unsolicited comes across to me as insecure. Their need to have everyone see salvation the way they do reveals some deeper shaky ground. Over on the more functional side of this line is the person who offers a look through a door, take it or leave it.

I remember a time eating alone in a Middle Eastern restaurant in Melbourne—basic, no-frills décor, plastic tables and chairs, really delicious food. Three men in their thirties came in to dine also. We were the only patrons at the time. I acknowledged them with a smile and a nod as they sat at the table next to mine. Before too long, the chatty one of them was striking up a conversation with me, while the other two were more interested in ordering and then eating their food.

As it turned out, they were quite devout, religious fellas. Islam was their discipline. The chatty one had obviously only recently found Allah, and his two "brothers" seemed to have grown up in Muslim families. The chatty bloke very quickly became determined to save my soul. He was telling me that unless I too "saw the light" and became a Muslim, I would remain an infidel and be damned. The endearing thing was that he was coming from a place of genuine care, albeit fear-based rather than love. He was determined to help me, but his fanaticism only served to repel.

The other two men, with their softer, more unassuming demeanor, were certainly more attractive versions of that particular "path to happiness." If I had been looking for suggestions, I would have been way more likely to seek them from the two not trying to convince me/scare me/convert me.

The point is, you can only teach someone something if they want you to. That being said, once the initial prerequisite has been established, share away!

If you ever find yourself getting excited and sharing something you've just come across before you've had a chance to even practice it yourself, it may be harder to teach. You might find yourself stumbling around the theory and not communicating it as clearly as could be. It's certainly easier to teach something after you've been practicing it.

Even then, the first time you teach it may still feel clumsy. That's okay. I find it helpful to let the others know if it's kinda new to me, and ask them to excuse me if I trip over a little in the sharing. Each time you teach it or use it as a tool with other people, it gets a little bit easier. After some time, it becomes second nature, and then you notice the practice you've been teaching/sharing has become a habitual part of your life.

~~~

Let's take an example from this book. Say you wanted to teach someone the CIA acronym from Chapter Three and how to use it. Someone says to you, "Hey, I've noticed how calm you've been for a while. It seems like you don't stress over things as much as you used to." Then they ask, "How do you do it?"

"Well, it comes from this really straightforward acronym I read in a book. The acronym is CIA."

"What does it stand for?"

"C stands for control. If you're worried about something and it's completely in your control, then do what you can to make it better. I stands for influence. If something is not in your control, but you have some influence over it, then give it the appropriate amount of your worry. Then, lastly, there are things we can't control or influence, so they go straight in the last category, A for accept. If something goes in the accept basket, it gets zero worry, concern, or stress."

Just like that, you became the teacher. If you are someone who feels more comfortable thinking of yourself as a "sharer," all good. It's not the title that matters. What counts is that you contributed by sharing something useful with someone who was curious and wanted to know.

Chapter Nineteen

WHAT IS OUR RESPONSIBILITY?

I s there a whisper inside you, any part of you, that wants to leave life better than you found it, to have some sort of positive impact? For some, it's a roar: a loud, driving power from within to do what they can to make the world a better place. For others, it may be as simple and pure as raising good children, equipping them as best as possible to have happy and healthy lives, and hopefully, just maybe, to play a positive role themselves in some way.

Perhaps for you, it's to lead a small team of people who find meaning in their work, or to create freedom from financial struggle, provide security and lifestyle for your partner, to make life just a bit easier.

Quite often, this drive comes after the basic me-centric survival needs are met. Once you are earning enough money to live and feel secure, there can arise a yearning to make it all "mean more."

Do you feel a version of this internal drive? Do you want to live a meaningful life? Whether it's micro and local, or macro and global (or anywhere in between), this inertia, this internal motivation to help make something better, is the drive of Evolution.

As an inseparable part of our species, the desire to seek to "improve" is ingrained. It's how we got to where we are. You can always fight it if you like. You could say, "I just don't care about making things better. I'm fine. I'm not hurting anyone. Why should I care whether [men/the climate/endangered species/ poverty/racial equality etc.] improve/s? It's not up to me to do anything about that."

But please beware. If your life is meaningless, if you feel there's no point, other than just to "enjoy yourself" or even just to "get by," there is every chance you will be left feeling empty at the very least. This can lead to a "numbness," to an apathetic disposition. This in turn is not only leaving you feeling detached, but also others not feeling attracted to you either. If you are in a relationship, over time, the sexual magnetism from you to your other half will fade. If you are single, you won't be shining and exuding that secret elixir of a "man on a mission." There is something organically attractive about a man driven by a purpose beyond himself.

Feeling like there is no point to anything beyond your own pleasures can also lead from detachment to depression. This pathway is certainly unpleasant and undesirable. It's obviously not the only cause of depression, there are many factors to that equation, but it is something to be conscious of, and can be flipped for use as a positive tool. For people who experience depression (whatever the reasons), the act of shifting their attention to contribution beyond themselves has been shown to offer relief from suffering. (A wonderfully well researched and informative read on this topic is Johann Hari's book *Lost Connections*.)

Find some meaning to life beyond yourself, find a cause you can contribute to and a way to consciously communicate that, and you will find a deeper happiness.

~~~

At the time of writing this book, horrible stories of male politicians here in Australia and their unacceptable misconduct toward female staff have been the focal point of mainstream media. I tend to avoid consuming mainstream news because largely the content for me is distasteful, sensationalized, and not my choice of where to put my attention, but in this case, it has my full support to be a national headline. Abuse, whether it be sexual, verbal, or purely physical, is utterly dysfunctional. And, as we've touched on in this book already, it is inflicted predominantly by men (the victims are both female and male).

Aha! A cause! The dysfunctional and inappropriate behavior of some males.

We should *all* be talking about this and doing what we can to address it.

You don't need to chain yourself to a tree to be "anti-deforestation" (for those of you who do, I love you and I am super glad you exist). You can choose recycled products and dispose of your waste thoughtfully. You don't have to wave a placard at a rally to demand racial equality (for those of you who do, I'm on your side). You can simply treat everyone equally and call a friend out when they don't—the latter part of that being very important.

What can you do, that sits within your authenticity, to help create change for the greater good? I am certainly not telling you what to do. There are countless numbers of ways to be a positive power for change. I am just saying that, believe it or not, one of the most important components of change is having conscious conversations about the issues.

What I am wanting to do in this chapter is pose some questions for you to ponder and offer some suggestions for ways you can be a part of change.

As a man, do you feel okay about the destructive dysfunctionalities of men? How do you feel about the negative stereotypes?

As a man, do you think we, as a Collective of Men, should improve, grow, and evolve?

As an individual, do you believe you have any capacity to be more active in this endeavor?

Thought Experiment

Imagine this: you are at a community fair, and there is a group activity taking place—the good old tug-o'-war. One big piece of rope and about a hundred people on one side of the line and a hundred on the other, all heaving and sweating and straining to pull the opposition over the line.

It's a stalemate. No movement either way. Two hundred people giving it everything they've got. What would one extra person do? Probably nothing against all that, you think to yourself. But, like a swinging vote, if you picked a side and joined in, all two hundred and one of you would start moving in the direction you chose!

What is the direction of our men's path you choose? Are you going to grab the rope? You can be anywhere on the scale between the poles from "this is my life's mission" through to just putting one hand on that rope and gently leaning in the right direction. That's up to you.

I reckon if you get involved in some way, it'll be a win-win; good for the greater good *and* good for you. Playing a part, big or small, in helping to rewrite the stereotypes of men, will be enriching your experience of life as well.

Okay, so how?

Choices. Small. Conscious. Gutsy. Choices.

Here are some made-up examples of situations where you could grab the rope and lean in the right direction.

SCENARIO 1, OPTION A

"Mate, did you see that rugby player on the news get in trouble for saying he was gonna go 'pull something—anything will do' down at the pub?" (Referring to having sex with a female—any female.)

"Yeah, I saw that. Pretty sure he was only joking. Ease up on him, wouldn't ya reckon?"

"Yeah, absolutely, fair fuckin' go, he didn't mean disrespect."

SCENARIO 1, OPTION B

"Mate, did you see that rugby player on the news get in trouble for saying he was gonna go 'pull something—anything will do' down at the pub?"

"Yeah, I saw that. He probably didn't mean disrespect, but I reckon it's shit the way he objectified women."

"Whaddya mean? He was just trying to have a laugh!"

"Yeah, I know, but I reckon there's other things we can laugh about without being disrespectful to women."

And the conversation then continues wherever it does from there. The point is that now there *is* a conversation about it, not just complicit approval and a head-in-the-sand-carry-on-as-you-were situation.

SCENARIO 2, OPTION A

"Hey, I think Frank is hitting the booze pretty hard at the moment. You know how angry he gets. Do ya reckon he's getting violent at home again?"

"I dunno. None of my business. I hope not."

"Yeah, me too. Pretty shit for Liz and the kids."

"Like I said, mate, what goes on behind closed doors ain't for us to go getting nosey about."

"Yeah, I guess so."

SCENARIO 2, OPTION B

"Hey, I think Frank is hitting the booze pretty hard at the moment. You know how angry he gets. Do ya reckon he's getting violent at home again?"

"Shit, I hope not. Liz got really hurt last time."

"Do ya reckon we should check in with him? See if we can help him through it?"

"I feel bad being nosey in other people's business, but he is our mate. I'm sure he would regret it if he lost his shit again."

"I'll give him a buzz, see if we can get together and talk about it."

"Yeah, okay. It'll be tricky to talk about, but if we let him know it's just because we care, it might be okay. We have to at least try."

SCENARIO 3, OPTION A

"Hey, mate, a few of us are heading out for a bite to eat tonight. Wanna come?"

"Nah, thanks, mate, I've got crook guts at the moment. Don't feel great. I'm just gonna head home." (Sub-text—I'm suffering anxiety at the moment. It twists up my insides, and I'm worried about what people will think.)

"Oh, c'mon. You haven't been out for ages. Suck it up. Just come out."

"Nah, fuck off. Leave me alone. I'm heading home. See ya tomorrow."

SCENARIO 3, OPTION B

"Hey, mate, a few of us are heading out for a bite to eat tonight. Wanna come?"

"I'd love to, but I've been having these kind of panic attacks lately, some kind of anxiety, and I don't want to be around people."

"Oh shit, really? That's no good, mate, I get that sometimes, it freaks me out. Are you okay?"

"Yeah, kind of. I don't really talk about it with anyone."

"Hey, I got put on to this psychologist last year. She really helped me with some strategies to make it easier. Would you like her number?"

"Man, that would actually be awesome. I've been too ashamed to bring it up, you know, didn't want to make a big deal out of it."

"You know, I reckon heaps more of us blokes go through this than you think. We should talk about it more."

By sharing these scenarios, I'm hoping you can think of similar (or different) situations that arise in your life where you could choose an "option B." I think you might be surprised by how well it's received. It is these little micro choices, these minor adjustments, that over the course of time, with the exponential effect of contagious positive behavior, will actually create change.

Chapter Twenty

CREATING THE NEXT GEN OF CONSCIOUS MEN

Parenting has been simultaneously the most rewarding and the most challenging experience of my life. And it continues to be that way, more now than ever, with seventeen- and fifteen-year-old sons who are very quickly becoming young men. Pretty early into this journey, I realized not only could I forgive my parents for anything I had previously resented, but beyond that, there was not even a need to "forgive." I mean, forgive them for what? Being human? Trying their best? Sometimes getting it right and other times messing it up? Each of us, in any moment, is only behaving to the best of our ability given the resources available to us at the time.

We are all perfectly imperfect. We are all the result of everything that led us to being who we are, at this moment in time. If my dad had known how to not lose his shit and throw me round that bedroom, he wouldn't have done it.

We parents aren't given a foolproof operation manual when we become parents. No matter how many books or resources we read, we still find ourselves in moments, tearing our hair out and thinking, *What the fuck am I supposed to do now?*

I have certainly lost track of the number of times I've thought, *Shit, I could've handled that so much better*. It has been an ongoing practice to keep accepting my shortcomings, and even to accept the part I've unwittingly played in any of the psychological damage that has occurred to my boys along the way. No matter how hard we try as parents to be the best we can be, our young people lose their innocence and develop their own cynicisms and limiting beliefs, one way or another.

We can choose to either beat ourselves up for our mistakes in the past, or learn from them, seek to heal the relationships with our kids in the present, and aim to be "better" as parents in the future. It's never too late to have conscious conversations with our children. I had some of the best of them with my dad in the last few years before he died.

I am a long way from being a "perfect" parent (and I'm not sure that's even definable), but I am doing the perfect job of being me, with all my imperfections. I am partially responsible for the adults my children are becoming, and it's also largely out of my control. I find myself using the CIA acronym and process described in this book *a lot* with parenting. Constantly realigning my expectations with reality and adjusting my worry and stress levels to come closer to the actual amount of influence I have in given situations. If you are a parent, I bet you get what a balancing act this is!

There is obviously a certain amount of nature that plays into the mix with nurture to result in who our children are and continue to become. Humans are born with certain genetic and behavioral tendencies, and obviously the environment we arrive in as babies, and subsequently grow up in, plays a part as well.

My two boys are like chalk and cheese behaviorally, despite coming from the same genetic history. The older of the two likes to follow the rules and stay out of trouble. He is risk-averse and happily cautious. He prefers the quality company of only a few people, loves his time alone at home, and cherishes the hours he chooses to spend with his grandmother and two-year-old cousin (we live communally in two farmhouses on a coastal sheep farm). As I mentioned in an earlier chapter, his lead behavioral style is C with a strong S blend.

The other lad is gregarious and sociable, making friends with many, and spending as much time as possible active out in the world. He breaks rules. He is driven by the need to "win." He pushes the boundaries whether he is skateboarding, surfing, or challenging authority. At the time of writing this, he had just turned fifteen, so throw that age factor into the mix and you might start to imagine some of the current parental challenges his mum and I are navigating. It's easy to see his strong *D* behavioral style showing up.

Despite the differing behavioral styles of our kids, there are some basic values parents try to impart to all their children. These are the values the parent believes in. At the core of the motivation to do this, we want to not only ensure their survival, but hopefully set them up to thrive and have a wonderful, happy life. This is, of course, natural. We feel they should adopt our values, because that's the way we've made sense of the world, and our kids are "our creation" after all, right? They represent us! (Oooh dear, slippery ego slope!)

Because these values are very close to our heart, and intertwined with our sense of identity, when our kids "buck the system" and behave in ways we think they shouldn't, it can really rock our internal boat.

Some of my top core values are kindness, compassion, and communication. When I see one of my kids being unkind, for example, it is extremely upsetting. On the surface level, I say to them, "The reason I want you to be kind is because it's a better way to be. It will set you up to have a much better life." But beneath that, my ego is flipping out, confusing who they are with who I am, taking their behavior personally, and reacting as if its (the ego's) own integrity is in peril.

Our children are not us. The "separation individuation" process children go through to become their own person has to be experienced by the parent as well.

Remember the concentric rings around your core relationship? Our children are *very* close to that core, and therefore, present possibly the most challenging relationship for communication at times. They did, after all, begin their lives as a part of us, literally, and so the unravelling of the psychological and energetic intertwinement is a tricky exercise. Lots of deep breaths. Lots of letting go.

~~~

One of the most important things to me as a parent has been that my boys feel like they can tell me anything. Open communication. So far, so good. I know it will be necessary for their development to have some things they don't tell me, but generally, they feel safe to be honest with me, and they pretty much tell me everything.

This, of course, comes with its challenges, because I know what they are up to, and perhaps sometimes I could almost prefer the bliss of ignorance! But this is far outweighed by the benefit of them feeling safe to talk about anything with their dad: what they are trying to figure out, feel or navigate, experiment with or understand, as they move through the teenage times of massive change and discovery.

As much as my parents loved me, I never had this with them. Certainly not with my dad, and only slightly more with my mum.

As the oldest of four siblings, I also didn't have someone paving the way, testing the waters. The more daunting "firsts" for me were solo and secret. Losing my virginity. Smoking weed. Piercing my ear (a bit harder to keep secret!). Stealing alcohol from Dad's bar and getting drunk. Sneaking out of my bedroom window to go and wander the streets with mates in the wee hours. Making a fake ID to sneak into bars and clubs when I was underage. Hush hush, Jem, keep that to yourself.

So, I am trying a different program this generational time round. Some updated software. Am I parenting the "right way"? That's impossible, because there is no one right way. I am doing it the best way I know how, and I am trying to assist evolution by doing some things differently from my dad. He used to discipline us with smacks; I have never hit my kids. He used to shut down emotional or challenging conversations; I make time to sit down and encourage them.

Despite believing we can improve generationally, I don't feel any judgement of those who have walked before us. In fact, it's quite the opposite. I respect all previous parents (even the dysfunctional ones who "knew no better") as the necessary evolutionary steps before us.

My hope is that conscious communication becomes just a part of the way my kids roll. I'm hoping they become men who can communicate openly and sensitively with their partners. I hope they speak kindly to themselves and communicate with their inner emotional worlds. I hope they seek to resolve things with words and listening. I'm hoping that, by being themselves, they will encourage, inspire, and allow other men to keep moving into their potential too.

I have all these hopes, yet I know there will be times to let the hopes go and simply accept what is. They are becoming the men they are becoming. I will continue to lean in as their dad and give this parenting caper everything I've got. And, at the same time, I must continue to let these young men go every day as well. They are journeying the way they are.

A promise I made to my boys when they were younger was that, if they were ever concerned about something, even if it was something they had done, if they came and talked with me about it, I wouldn't get angry. If consequences were required, they would be there, but I would stay calm. I've almost managed to adhere to that promise. Enough that they both trust they can come to me. It's interesting that they worry more about me "losing my shit" than they do about the consequences.

It seems reasonably common for teenage boys to go through an extended period of time, perhaps years, of communicating in grunts. Grunts and one-word answers. This is okay. It must be kinda normal, because I remember being there myself. I don't believe, however, that the grunts are a representation of the dialogue that's going on internally for them. It seems to be more of a lack of inclination to share. I'm sure there are rivers of thoughts and emotions flowing through their consciousness in more complex forms than just "Yep," or "Nup," or "Meh."

When I manage to get a conversation going that they are interested in, voila!! The expression through coherent and constructed sentences flows again! (I don't do this all the time. Sometimes their one-word answers to Dad's questions are fine.)

I'm finding that a good way into conversation with both of them is through asking about the things they are into. Seeking to understand what they care about. When they've spent a few hours learning a new skateboard trick, I'll ask for the blow-by-blow story of how they got there. When I see them really engaged with something on YouTube, I ask them to share with me what they like about it. Sometimes I'll come into a silence by offering "A penny for your thoughts." I am curious what they're thinking about, what consumes their inner attention.

Then there's the times they are curious about me. "Have you tried [_____], Dad?" "Have you ever done [_____], Dad?" It's tricky knowing how much of my past to share with them and when. I've lived a reasonably wild life at times, and one certainly has to measure the appropriate timing for things to be revealed! (Eeek—there's that balance between lying and being too honest before it's appropriate!)

The on-the-spot decisions start early on with things like, "Dad, tell me the truth... Is Santa Claus real?" Then the topics and decisions gain gravity from there. All parents have to navigate their version of fantasy, honesty, white lies, and home truths. As with other aspects of parenting, there is no "one best way." There is just the way you decide to do it in each of those moments when you get caught by surprise.

Oh, shit, I'm having that conversation with my kid! I was wondering when this was going to happen. Damn, I've had no time to prepare. Yikes. okay, I'm just gonna say [   ].

I think what's more important than whether you say the "right" thing at the "right" time is that we encourage conversation with our kids and continue to do so all the way through into their adulthood. Obviously, this is important for all kids, but specific to this book is the importance of it for our boys and young men.

As I've mentioned previously, conscious communication (although not the only necessary factor or ingredient) is a vital component for helping to create the next generation of men: men who will be less likely to resort to violence; men who respect women; men who understand their own emotions and how to communicate them; men who can support each other in their vulnerabilities and challenges; men who can shoulder responsibility and are happy to take appropriate action.

For this to happen, our young males need to know it's natural to communicate. They need to know that true strength isn't a façade of stiff-upper-lip; it's the courage to have integrity, keep walking through uncertainty, *and* to talk about their challenges. They need to see that communicating with their mates about deeper stuff is a sign of true friendship. They need to know that "leaning in" to the emotional conversations with their partner is a sign of love.

I know this all sounds lofty and ideal, and it is, but if we are not striving for a better way, we're not likely to improve. It's important for our boys to know the right direction when aiming for manhood. It's helpful for them to have a GPS guiding system provided by their parents, especially by their dads, and hopefully other men in their community. This navigation system works with examples and communication. Mind you, sometimes, in the short term, the system may not seem to be working. There are speed humps and local setbacks on a boy's journey, but there is also hope that over the longitude of a bigger picture, the general direction will prevail, and our next generation, our boys, will become better men.

It is this hope I hold on to, as I am challenged by the curve balls having teenage boys brings. The behaviors I have been passionately advocating and displaying to my sons are sometimes thrown to the gutter in the apparent defiance of the Righteous Youth. Then there I am, exasperated, frustrated, and disappointed. Breathe, Jem, pause, observe, and become mindful. (This actually works.)

Despite the testosterone-fueled troubles one of my boys is creating for himself now, at the age of fifteen, I have to believe that, with GPS consistency and communication over time, the foundations formed will one day support a structure with functional integrity. I have to hope, in the years to come, his "wayward" times become memories and campfire stories. Look me up ten years after the publication of this book and I'll let you know how it went!

Chapter Twenty-One

TIMING

I was solo. Happy. Independent, yet strangely connected with the thousand other people packed into the auditorium. Strangers and kindred spirits. A hush gently settled through us all, like the breath of a blanket, tucking us in warm and safe as we anticipated the next keynote speaker.

Day two of the Mindful Leader Global Forum in Sydney, Australia. My notebook was brimming with takeaways and lightbulb moments, like harvested thoughts ready to be milled into grain. But I'd been here before: conference attendee, determined and inspired by great people yet again. So many awesome learnings in years gone by and so few of them adopted, implemented, and habitualized. Would it be different this time? Would something land? Would I leave and make a change?

Although the next keynote speaker was physically a small man—dwarfed by the enormous stage he made his way onto and the massive screen onto which he was projected for all to see—his stature and composure emanated the quiet and modest confidence of a great, wise sage. You could've heard a pin drop in the silences between his steps across the boards.

To this day, I remember clearly two of the things he said: "Know the work and *do* the work," and "Pause often." For some reason, it was just the right time for me to be in that room, to be affected by this man and to hear those two simple pieces of advice. I listened. I took action. I changed. The timing was right.

~~~

"Do the work" simply meant "live the practice." In this case it was meditation. Don't just understand it conceptually. Meditate. Regularly. Forever. As with breathing, drinking, and eating, meditating and integrating mindfulness daily is now a way of life.

"Pause often" has become one of the most deceptively simple and effective habits to form. So much so that I share this teaching with all of my clients, from CEOs to small business owners, across all sectors from government to not-for-profit. I teach it in my online courses and encourage it with my kids. When you are in the middle of doing something, or between tasks, or on your way somewhere...pause. Just for a few seconds. Become mindful; observe what you can notice: your breath, any sounds, your heartbeat, your thoughts...and then continue.

This micro-recalibration takes no time at all, but with practice becomes your instant access pass to equanimity. I find it particularly useful when I'm running late or getting flustered.

~~~~

My hope for you is that this was the right time for you to find this book. Rather than just another read, with some ideas or stories that resonated, perhaps you will decide to adopt an idea or understanding and implement a new practice.

You either will or you won't, and whichever way you go, what will be for you, is then what's meant to be. If you do make changes in the way you go about life, this will affect change in life around you as well. Positive ripples are a wonderful thing.

Remember it starts with you. The communication you have with yourself. Remember to choose quality words for your internal dialogue. Take time to nurture this relationship. Become familiar with and forgiving of your internal world. You can calm your sea.

Loosen your grip on how you think things should be. When you have nothing to defend, you cannot be attacked. Navigating your way through any storm can either be fighting the elements or harnessing them. The latter requires flexibility and the courage to let go of your predetermined course.

Seek to understand and therefore honor others in their differences. Beneath the surface of culture, behavior, and opinions, there are some very common elements to our human experience. These commonalities can bridge the gaps and pave the way for better conversations.

Lastly, when you can remember to be mindful of the higher purpose before (or in the midst of) any communication, you will remain more conscious. From this place, you will serve the greater good and be more likely to influence a positive outcome.

As communication is the key to our relationships, and the tool with which we make manifest our dreams, improving your ability here is improving your experience of life.

Thank you for taking the time to read this book. I wish you well on your journey, wherever it may take you. And may you be an inspiration, inadvertently or intentionally, for other men along the way.

The End

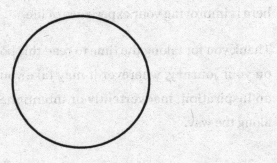

&
The Beginning

Resources

The Five Love Languages, Gary Chapman

The Critically Reflective Practitioner, Neil and Sue Thompson

The Untethered Soul, Michael Singer

The 7 Habits of Highly Effective People, Stephen Covey

Conscious, Annaka Harris

When, Daniel H. Pink

Psychological Types, Dr. Carl Jung

Emotions of Normal People, Dr. William Marston

Lost Connections, Johann Hari

The Way of the Superior Man, David Deida

Acknowledgments

The lessons I've learnt that have helped me on my journey to gradually becoming more conscious, and hopefully continually improving my ability to communicate, have come through many relationships, teachers, literature, life lessons, and time in contemplation. There are too many influences to list them all here, but I would like to acknowledge some of the people closest to me, who have been instrumental in shaping this book.

To my late father, Dave, and brother, Tim—you were two of the most influential people in my life. You both dying within months of each other—back at the time of 2009 becoming 2010—marked the end of what our family was, and the beginning of what it is. I love you both completely, think of you daily, and continue to learn from who you were. You live on in us.

To my sons, Jedi and Noah. I am so proud of you both and the men you are becoming. You never asked for the trauma of your parents separating, or the inconvenience of living out of a suitcase and moving from house to house each week. You've adapted and adjusted and accepted. Being your father has been not only the most rewarding experience of my life, but perhaps the provider of the biggest learnings as well. Thank you for loving me always, even when I've tripped and stumbled in my parenting. I see you. I hear you. I love you.

To Lakotah and Quinlan, thank you for opening your hearts to me and gradually allowing me into your lives. As with my boys, you didn't ask for all the change, the coming together, the blending of our families, but you stayed the course, and I feel very loved by you both. Learning to communicate in our relationships is something I am very grateful for. I will always be here for you.

Dearest Mum, Gabriel, I wouldn't swap you for the world or change a single thing about you. You continue to inspire not only me, but countless others who know you and love you. A truly humble matriarch, with a most generous heart and determined spirit. Thank you for everything.

Sister Beth and brother Chelli, we know how ridiculously wonderful our relationships are. To have siblings who are also dearest friends is truly something worthy of the awareness and gratitude we continue to communicate. Unconditional love.

Lastly, to my beautiful woman, my life partner, my soul mate and best friend, Talia. You know everything I feel about you and the entity that is Us. I quite simply wouldn't be the man I am today without the growth that has occurred through the intimacy, the safety, the honesty in our communication, and the tenderness in the way we love each other. Spending my life with you makes everything else a bonus, icing on the cake. I love you completely, deeply, and very happily. May we grow to ripe, old ages by each other's side with lots of grandkids (and great grandkids!) coming to visit. ☺

About the Author

Jem Fuller has led a very colorful life. From years of barefoot backpacking around the Indian subcontinent to senior leader with a multinational company, he has been to the extremes.

Jem has worked as a reflexologist, Chinese masseur, Reiki practitioner, kindergarten teacher in Asia, global tattooist, fire dancer, motorcycle courier, actor, singer/songwriter, travel consultant, and, prior to commencing his coaching practice, in senior corporate leadership.

Since 2013, Jem has been coaching and facilitating for CEOs and senior leaders across the government, private, not-for-profit, and health sectors. He is also the founding director and facilitator of his own international leadership retreat company, taking leaders away on Conscious Leader programs to the remote Indian Himalaya, jungles of northern Bali, and deserts of Australia.

Jem is a dedicated partner and father, who loves spending time in nature camping, hiking, and surfing. He loves writing songs and making music. He values connection, compassion, kindness, and generosity.

You can access Jem's online courses in meditation, resilience, personal development, and communication via his website, www.jemfuller.com. You can also download his e-books, subscribe to his newsletters, or watch his TEDx talk from the same site.

Mango Publishing, established in 2014, publishes an eclectic list of books by diverse authors—both new and established voices—on topics ranging from business, personal growth, women's empowerment, LGBTQ studies, health, and spirituality to history, popular culture, time management, decluttering, lifestyle, mental wellness, aging, and sustainable living. We were named 2019 *and* 2020's #1 fastest growing independent publisher by *Publishers Weekly*. Our success is driven by our main goal, which is to publish high-quality books that will entertain readers as well as make a positive difference in their lives.

Our readers are our most important resource; we value your input, suggestions, and ideas. We'd love to hear from you—after all, we are publishing books for you!

Please stay in touch with us and follow us at:

Facebook: Mango Publishing
Twitter: @MangoPublishing
Instagram: @MangoPublishing
LinkedIn: Mango Publishing
Pinterest: Mango Publishing
Newsletter: mangopublishinggroup.com/newsletter

Join us on Mango's journey to reinvent publishing, one book at a time.